The Struggle Is Real

Participant's Guide

The Struggle is Real.

Participant's Guide

Nicole Unice

TYNDALE
MOMENTUM®

*The nonfiction imprint of
Tyndale House Publishers, Inc.*

Visit Tyndale online at www.tyndale.com.

Visit Tyndale Momentum online at www.tyndalemomentum.com.

Visit Nicole Unice at nicoleunice.com.

TYNDALE, *Tyndale Momentum*, and Tyndale's quill logo are registered trademarks of Tyndale House Publishers, Inc. The Tyndale Momentum logo is a trademark of Tyndale House Publishers, Inc. Tyndale Momentum is the nonfiction imprint of Tyndale House Publishers, Inc., Carol Stream, Illinois.

The Struggle Is Real Participant's Guide: A Six-Week Study

Designed by Jennifer Phelps

The author is represented by Chip MacGregor of MacGregor Literary, Inc.

For information about special discounts for bulk purchases, please contact Tyndale House Publishers at csresponse@tyndale.com, or call 1-800-323-9400.

ISBN 978-1-4964-2752-6

Printed in the United States of America

24	23	22	21	20	19	18
7	6	5	4	3	2	1

Contents

A Word to Participants

If you've picked up this guide, some part of you resonates with the idea that the struggle is real.

At least we're starting with honesty!

I don't know what struggle is at the forefront of your mind and heart right now. It might be the struggle between you and someone you love. It might be an unexpected and unwelcome challenge involving your health, job, or finances. It might simply be the struggle to get up every morning, pay the bills, feed the kids, walk the dog, and try to find time to exercise while still making room in your day to do your devotions, love your spouse, and pray with your kids at night. Probably it's a deep-down angst—the struggle between your ideal life and your reality. But hey, here's the good news: The struggle most certainly *is* real, *and* the struggle can be good.

This participant's guide is a companion to the six-session video curriculum *The Struggle Is Real DVD Experience*. My hope is that you'll use both this guide and the video series either on your own for self-study or in a small group, with a book club, or with another circle of friends who want to make sense of their lives in the bigger story of God's freedom and grace.

Over the next six sessions, we'll explore how our struggles are part of the bigger story that goes all the way back to Adam and Eve—and how we can find God's wisdom so that we can rewrite that story into a wholehearted life. The study is meant to complement the book *The Struggle Is Real*. I think you'll enjoy these sessions most if you read the book as well, but you can also complete the study using just the participant's guide and the video.

My prayer for you over the coming weeks is that you experience the freedom that comes from self-awareness and God-awareness and from recognizing the beautiful way that God meets you in the struggle with His grace, truth, and mercy.

Here are some answers to FAQs to help get you started:

What do I need to complete this study?

You'll need the *Participant's Guide* and a Bible along with the video sessions. We also recommend *The Struggle Is Real* book, but it is not required for the study.

The book *The Struggle Is Real* is like a personal conversation in which I draw from my own life and the lives of others who've shared their stories of coming into wholehearted connection with Christ. This participant's guide takes those truths and makes them personal and interactive as we open the Bible together and walk through some life-changing principles. The videos center around a few stories from friends of mine who've experienced what it means to walk in God's freedom, along with my teaching straight from the Bible, in order to help you understand and apply God's wisdom and promises to your daily life.

You may choose to read *The Struggle Is Real* first and then reinforce your learning with the study, or you can read the book as a companion to the study. (At the start of each session's On Your Own section, I recommend which chapters from the book to read that week.) You can also do the study without reading the book. It is best, however, to use the participant's guide *with* the video, as those two are designed to work together.

Should I complete this study on my own or with a group?

The curriculum may be completed on your own or with a group. You may need or want to work through this material independently, and you can certainly do that. In that case, "being together" will be a conversation between the two of us, as we do the work of inviting God into your story and seeing Him change your perspective as you spend time in His Word.

If you have the opportunity to study this material with others—whether one friend or a crowd of one hundred—I recommend that approach. I've found that one of God's greatest gifts is the chance to experience fellowship through the encouragement of being together.

Scripture is clear that we are called to share each other's burdens, and that in doing so, we fulfill the law of Christ

(Galatians 6:2). God designed us to grow in community. When we circle up, whether in a group of two or twelve, we are acknowledging that we need one another for faith, for encouragement, and for the accountability needed to live with love and intentionality—not just for ourselves, but for others.

The book of Hebrews says that we should run the race of life with perseverance *because* we have such a great cloud of witnesses around us testifying to the love of Christ (see 12:1). Those witnesses include the generations of faithful men and women who have gone before us and the generation we are part of now. That means that your life—the way God has rescued you from your own sin, the way God can restore and redeem your hardest struggles—is a part of His great and glorious story.

Studying God's Word with others is a reminder that your connection to Christ is also a connection to other people. It's okay if you feel unsure in your faith. God has given you His Word, a sure and steady anchor. And He's given you others—people you can link arms with to gain the strength and support you need to live boldly into your new story.

I'm considering leading a group; how can you help?

Whether you're a veteran small group leader or are ready to jump in with some friends and lead a group for the first time, I want to help! Turn to page 141 to access the leader's guide and helpful hints, as well as individual session outlines for each week.

How long should each session take to complete?

Each session is structured so that it can be completed in ninety minutes. You can take longer if needed, but I've found that most people's attention begins to wane at this point. If you have less time, you can edit the questions and move more of the group work to participants' personal study time.

If you are studying on your own, it will take less time to work through the videos (about fifteen to twenty minutes) and the Bible study (about thirty minutes).

In addition, working through this guide involves about fifteen minutes of daily work (five days a week) to help you get into the habit of reading God's Word on a regular basis. If you haven't yet developed the habit of spending time with God, I encourage you to remove one distraction from your day and replace that time with this book's daily work for the duration of the study. You'll need a Bible and something to write with—there's room to record your reflections right in the participant's guide.

What do all the icons within the sessions mean?

Throughout the sessions, you'll see helpful icons to guide your journey and help you get oriented, whether you are studying on your own or with a group.

Icon Legend

Focus Point
This introduces the key phrase from each session.

Video
This tells you when to tune in to the video component.

Reflection/Application
The Reflection and Application questions allow you to take stock of what you are learning that week.

In the Word
This indicates when you'll spend time in Scripture alongside the video material, whether individually or in your group.

Daily
Each week includes five sections for fifteen-minute engagement in the material, to keep you growing throughout the week.

Group
If you are a group leader, look for this icon in the Leader's Guide (which begins on page 141) for ideas on how to facilitate each session.

Okay, new friend, one more thing—I'd love to hear from you! If you'd like to share how *The Struggle Is Real* has impacted your life or group, let me know. You can reach me through social media or at nicoleunice.com.

I am excited for you as you begin this exploration of God's wisdom for your everyday struggles in life. I think you'll find that though your struggle is very real—God's love for you is very deep, His freedom for you is vast, and His wisdom for you can change your perspective on the past and future chapters in your story.

The struggle is the start of the story. But it's certainly not the end. Let's jump in!

Much love,
Nicole

The Struggle Is Real ...and Good

The story line that we've bought about life—the one that says if it's not easy, it's not good—is a lie.

The Struggle Is Real, chapter 2, page 35

Struggles are not fun. They are not glamorous. They are not easy. But that doesn't make them bad. From cover to cover, the Bible is open about our raw reality in the struggle. Scripture is filled with stories about the beautiful results created from the struggle; the intangible and eternal things learned in the struggle; and the people we can become through the struggle. Let's look together at what our struggles teach us about life, about choices, and about the surprising role of wisdom in all of it.

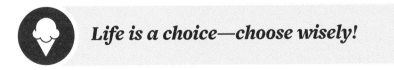

Life is a choice—choose wisely!

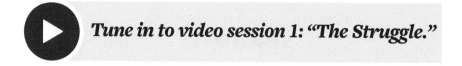

Tune in to video session 1: "The Struggle."

Video Notes

Wisdom provides clarity in a confusing world.

Fearing God is not about punishment; it's about love.

We have a choice to make about the story we believe.

Liz's Story

"I had to surrender all of my fears and all of my worries to God's best for me. And it wasn't until I did . . . that things really changed for me. The more I leaned into God and trusted Him for every aspect of my life, the more joy I felt."

Reflection

1. On your own or with your group, reflect on one thing from Liz's story or Nicole's teaching that you needed to hear today.

2. What choices did Liz make in difficult times that changed her perspective? As you consider difficult situations or relationships in your life, where would you most like to adopt a new outlook or attitude?

3. Think of the challenges you faced today. Using the graph below, mark how likely you are to invite God into those struggles.

Totally
Likely

Not at All
Likely

4. I believe there are times when any of us might answer "not at all likely" to the idea of inviting God into our struggles. Circle which of the following factors might keep you from inviting God in:

- My struggles feel too petty to pray about.
- I'm too preoccupied or busy to stop and ask God into them.
- I don't know how to pray about these things.
- I used to pray about these things but didn't feel like I got any answers from God.
- Other:

 ## In the Word

Let's look closely at three Bible passages that provide the foundation for understanding why God's wisdom is so important for our lives.

1. Turn to Proverbs 3:13-18. This section uses vivid imagery to describe the role of wisdom in our lives. Record one or two phrases from the passage that stand out to you:

-

-

2. Now turn to Proverbs 4:5-7 and 20-23. Notice the urgent tone in this chapter. What does the author say are the results of having wisdom? What might that look like in today's world?

3. The New Testament book of James was written by the brother of Jesus. In this letter, James gives instruction for living with wisdom—by understanding the truth of our lives in Christ and then acting on it. Faith is not meant to be an abstract concept in our minds. It's a true, living reality that should play out in our daily lives.

    Read James 3:13-18. Write a list of the characteristics of wisdom:

    -                       •

    -                       •

    -                       •

    -                       •

Application

How would you explain what you've learned about wisdom and how to apply it to your own life? Here's a prompt to get you started:

> Wisdom is _____, and it matters for my
> life because _____.

During this week's Daily Study, we'll continue to lay the foundation for understanding the power and relevancy of wisdom for our lives. We'll then spend the next few weeks understanding how wisdom works to redefine our relationship with God and with others, which enables us to live out our days with confidence and joy.

Remember, James tells us, "If any of you lacks wisdom, you should ask God, who gives generously to all without finding fault" (James 1:5).

A prayer for you:

*Father, as we begin to look more closely at how
Your wisdom directs our struggles, help us to trust
in Your promises and believe that they are for each
of us—in the life we are living right now. Amen!*

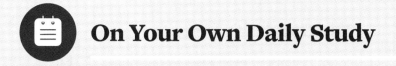

On Your Own Daily Study

THIS WEEK'S RECOMMENDED READING:
Chapters 1 and 2 in The Struggle Is Real

As we turn to God's Word together each day, we have the opportunity to reorient our perspective of ourselves, others, and God. My prayer for you is that you discover how eminently practical and completely essential time in the Word is for redefining the struggles of everyday life. This week, we'll turn our minds toward a vision of what the "good life" can look like when we live in Christ.

Day One
Searching for the Good Life

RECOMMENDED BIBLE READING:
Proverbs 3:1-18

The first chapter in *The Struggle Is Real* contains a baseline questionnaire called the Good Life Inventory, which allows us to assess how fully we are living into the wholehearted life God offers. Each of the descriptions on page 8 captures how the Bible describes the "good life"—living in God's way rather than our own.

We'll look at how each of these attributes is connected to wisdom throughout our daily exercises.

The Good Life Inventory

Think about the last two weeks. Put a check by the statements that currently describe you. Answer honestly—this is for your growth! The only way we grow is with honesty, and the only person you would be lying to is yourself. Be courageously honest.

1. I am totally committed to knowing the truth about myself. I am not afraid to ask others around me to help me see blind spots or trouble areas in my life.

2. I have a peaceful and nonanxious presence, both inside and out.

3. Generally I feel that my soul is untroubled and undisturbed. I have nothing to hide.

4. I regularly and sincerely ask for forgiveness from my family, friends, and coworkers.

5. I respect my own heart, body, and soul as something to be cherished.

6. I treat conflicting patterns of thinking and behaving in myself with gentleness.

7. I have a clear sense of purpose in my life.

8. I have experienced deep compassion for someone who has hurt me.

9. I feel total freedom from my past hurts and regrets.

10. I experience joy on a daily basis.

Each of these ten statements represents some aspect of what it means to be fully whole in every relationship—with God, with ourselves, with others, and with the world. In session 2, we'll talk about why those relationships fractured in the first place and how Christ works to redeem them in our lives. But before we seek to restore what has been broken, let's consider what it means to live as God intended for us—fully whole and fully free in our everyday living.

This week, we'll focus on the first three statements in the inventory:

+ I am totally committed to knowing the truth about myself. I am not afraid to ask others around me to help me see blind spots or trouble areas in my life.

+ I have a peaceful and nonanxious presence, both inside and out.

+ Generally I feel that my soul is untroubled and undisturbed. I have nothing to hide.

Each of these statements reflects a soul that is rigorously honest and refreshingly transparent—yet at the same time peaceful and secure. This is the outward expression of inward wisdom. Let's see what the Bible has to say about this kind of life:

Below is James 3:17-18 from three Bible translations. Read through each and circle or highlight all the attributes of a person living in God's wisdom ("the wisdom that comes from heaven"):

New International Version

The wisdom that comes from heaven is first of all pure; then peace-loving, considerate, submissive, full of mercy and good fruit, impartial and sincere. Peacemakers who sow in peace reap a harvest of righteousness.

New Living Translation

The wisdom from above is first of all pure. It is also peace loving, gentle at all times, and willing to yield to others. It is full of mercy and the fruit of good deeds. It shows no favoritism and is always sincere. And those who are peacemakers will plant seeds of peace and reap a harvest of righteousness.

Amplified Bible

The wisdom from above is first pure [morally and spiritually undefiled], then peace-loving [courteous, considerate], gentle, reasonable [and willing to listen], full of compassion and good fruits. It is unwavering, without [self-righteous] hypocrisy [and self-serving guile]. And the seed whose fruit is righteousness (spiritual maturity) is sown in peace by those who make peace [by actively encouraging goodwill between individuals].

1. How does this passage relate to the "Good Life" statements above?

2. As you go through your day, think about how "wisdom from heaven" shows up in your life—or doesn't! Here's a challenge for you (if you choose to accept it!): Lean into one or more of the attributes listed above as your goal for today.

3. Pay attention to your thoughts, feelings, and actions this week. Take note of whether you are committed to knowing the truth about yourself; whether you are generally peaceful and nonanxious; and whether you go about your days relatively untroubled with nothing to hide. We'll come back to this on Day 5.

Day Two
Inviting God into Your Struggle

RECOMMENDED BIBLE READING:
Proverbs 3:18-35

Most of us are aware that we live in the gap between our ideal (the good life) and our reality (the Struggle). In chapter 1, I identify this struggle as "the frustrating place between who I want to be and who I actually am." This might manifest itself in interrupting your "quiet time" by yelling at your kids, tackling a hard project and giving up in frustration twenty minutes later, or giving marriage advice to a friend and getting in a fight with your spouse that evening.

1. Name some of the relationships, circumstances, or thought patterns where this is true for you.

On page 3, we considered the prompt "Think of the challenges you faced today" and asked you to evaluate how likely you are to invite God into those struggles. Then we considered which of the following keep us from allowing God into those places:

- My struggles feel too petty to pray about.
- I'm too preoccupied/busy to stop and ask God into them.
- I don't know how to pray about these things.
- I used to pray about these things but didn't feel like I got any answers from God.
- Other:

As you think about the reason(s) you are reluctant to turn to God, consider what the Bible tells us about the struggle. Begin by reading Psalm 139:23-24.

2. What does the psalmist ask God to do?

3. What is the result?

When we invite God to examine the deepest parts of us, He will gently but honestly reveal our misconceptions, blind spots, and sin. Yet notice that when we open ourselves to God, He will also guide us onto the pathway of eternal, abundant life.

4. Next read Philippians 4:6-7. What does Paul (the writer of Philippians) instruct us to do?

5. What is the result?

6. Apparently, nothing is too small for God. He commands us to bring all our concerns—both small and large—to Him. In the process, He provides both defensive (He guards our hearts) and offensive (He leads us forward) help for our lives! Where do you need to trust God to guard and lead you?

Day Three
The Promise of Wisdom

RECOMMENDED BIBLE READING:
James 1:1-18

1. Turn to James 1:2-8. What promise is given in verse 5?

2. There is a condition on that promise in verse 6. What is it?

The *NIV Key Word Study Bible* defines the Greek word for doubt, *diakrino*, as "deciding between." When used in this verse in James, it denotes "to be divided in one's mind."

One of the key distinctions that Scripture makes is between being wholeheartedly with God or "double-minded." Our God is a loving God, but He is also an exclusive God. He wants our wholeheartedness, the complete attention of our heart, soul, mind, and strength (see Mark 12:30). With our wholehearted devotion comes the ability to examine ourselves honestly and to invite God into the struggle, no matter where we find it.

What if, whenever you faced a challenging, confusing, or frustrating situation, you asked God for His wisdom? What if you chose to pray *passionately* and *persistently*, believing that God is faithful, and that since He said He would give you wisdom, He will? Oh yes, "the fear of the Lord [believing He can and will do what He says] is the beginning of wisdom" (Proverbs 9:10).

3. Take a few minutes now to consider this passage and the James 3 passage from day 1. Ask God to bring to mind areas of your life that lack wisdom. List them below:

In closing, imagine offering up each of the words on this list to God with the assurance that He will answer.

Day Four
The Soil of Our Souls

RECOMMENDED BIBLE READING:
James 1:19-27

Author, blogger, and popular speaker Sally Clarkson has always loved gardening, and she expected to enjoy it more than ever when her family moved to their current home: "I was fooled into thinking gardening would be easy when we relocated to Colorado one spring. Myriad wildflowers swayed gracefully in the ballet of springtime breezes, charming me to my tiptoes as we moved into our home."[1] Before long, however, she made some painful discoveries. Not only was their home built on a mountainside teeming with hungry deer, but also the soil was rocky, which meant she had to carefully select the few plants that could thrive in such conditions.

Jesus used a similar story to explain why God's Word sometimes doesn't attach firmly to our hearts.

1. Turn to Matthew 13:3-9 and 18-23. In this parable, what does Jesus teach about why certain people take in God's Word but remain preoccupied with the cares of the world?

17

2. What is the result?

Our hearts, it turns out, need to establish deep roots in God's Word before they can produce a harvest of wisdom, peace, and right living. Here we see a place in our lives where the struggle may definitely be real. How we receive God's Word varies widely. When we find ourselves so busy, so worried, or so preoccupied that we don't find time for God, we are in danger of becoming like the seed that dries out or is choked out and never has a chance to grow.

3. When you hear God's Word, do you ever find that it is crowded out by other thoughts, priorities, or concerns? Explain.

4. What does James 1:21-25 tell us about how to access the power of the Word God has planted in your heart?

Day Five
Choose Wisely

RECOMMENDED BIBLE READING:
Deuteronomy 30:11-20

One of the greatest challenges in life is that of *choice*. Because God has given us freedom, every day we must decide whether to believe that God is good, whether to trust Him, and whether to surrender our lives to Him. This is not a choice we make once for all time, but one that requires a continued setting (and resetting) of our hearts each day.

1. Turn to Deuteronomy 30:19-20. In this context, it's obvious that Moses is talking about more than just biological life. What do you think it means to "choose life"? What does it look like for you to "choose life" today?

2. When you think about choosing life according to God's design, what do you want your life to have more of? What do you want your life to have less of?

3. Deuteronomy 30:20 describes three actions we can take to choose life. What are they? Which do you find most difficult?

4. On day 1 of this week's study, you were asked to observe yourself this week and consider whether you are committed to knowing the truth about yourself; whether you are generally peaceful and nonanxious; and whether you go about your days relatively untroubled with nothing to hide. What did you learn about yourself through this process?

Next week, we'll look at how we make sense of our personal story in the greater story God tells about us through the Bible. Buckle up, friends—it's going to be an incredible ride!

As you finish session 1, this is my prayer for you:

Father, there are so many areas in our lives where we might want to trust You, but the reality is, we don't. Treat us gently, as all good fathers would, and lead us into the truth of our doubt. Help us to be children who trust You, who love You, and who persevere in prayer with You, believing that You will provide the wisdom we seek. Amen!

Your Struggle Matters

The way people articulate the story of their lives has a great impact on their overall well-being. In one study, those who had the highest satisfaction with life and deepest commitment to others told their life story in a redemptive arc.

The Struggle Is Real, chapter 3, page 50

This week, we take a deep dive into our past to understand our present—and reset for our future. The struggle shows up in surprising places—and yet in the brokenness, we find the hope of the redemptive love of Christ.

 The struggle starts the story.

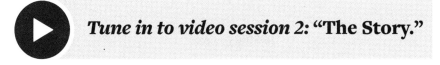

Tune in to video session 2: "The Story."

Video Notes

The way we remember yesterday profoundly shapes the choices we make today.

Our character is formed one moment at a time.

Our struggles point to deeply fractured places in our soul.

Serious problems need serious solutions.

Erin's Story

"Because I refused to challenge myself, I really didn't have eyes to see the way God wanted to use me in the lives of other people."

 **Reflection**

1. What is something that you heard in Nicole's teaching or Erin's story that sticks with you?

2. Can you think of a memory that influenced the way you interpret your life? It might be an example of good being used for evil, such as being told you were smart and then feeling pressure to be perfect, or of evil being used for good, such as losing a loved one but finding love and compassion in the midst of it.

3. Nicole spoke of the four-way brokenness of the world, beginning with the enemy's work of getting us to doubt the intentions of God. Have you ever resonated with any of the following whispers of doubt? Circle your answer below each statement:

God doesn't really need me for any big purpose—my life isn't that important.

I've struggled with this in the past.

I currently struggle with this.

I have never struggled with this.

God is distant and doesn't care about me.

I've struggled with this in the past.

I currently struggle with this.

I have never struggled with this.

God hasn't fixed my struggle/hurt/trouble, so I must not be worth it.

I've struggled with this in the past.

I currently struggle with this.

I have never struggled with this.

God is punishing me because I haven't been good enough.

I've struggled with this in the past.

I currently struggle with this.

I have never struggled with this.

I've been hurt in the past and God didn't help, so I'm on my own.

I've struggled with this in the past.

I currently struggle with this.

I have never struggled with this.

Others have it a lot worse than I do, so my problems don't need God's attention.

I've struggled with this in the past.

I currently struggle with this.

I have never struggled with this.

These are commonly held doubts about God's interest in and intentions toward us. Why do we all share similar doubts? The Bible has something to say about the origin of this kind of doubt, which is *exactly* what the struggle is about. Let's discover it together.

In the Word

For our time together in Scripture, let's seek to understand the Bible's way of showing how our everyday struggles all connect to the "capital-*s*" Struggle of sin. I've made it personal (uncomfortably personal!) here.

Write your own name at the beginning of the verse:

Colossians 1:21

_____, *once you were alienated from God and were enemies in your minds because of your evil behavior.*

Our first and primary brokenness comes from being separated from God by sin. But where did that "evil behavior" come from? Most of us don't spend much time thinking about how we've become who we are. Perhaps we've absorbed the message that it all comes from "within"—that our identity and potential are some mash-up of genetics, environment, and our own grit.

But the Bible tells a different story—a story of good and evil. People hold many different attitudes toward the role of evil in the world. You may find the idea of Satan scary or comical, or maybe you just don't think much about the idea at all. But for the sake of understanding, let's look at what Scripture has to say about Satan and then reorder our own understanding around that:

1. Turn to Genesis 3:1-3 and read the passage (even if you are alone, reading aloud may help you better understand its significance!). Now turn to Genesis 2:17 to cross-check Eve's words against what she'd been commanded. What's the difference?

2. Turn to Matthew 4:1-11. What tactics does Satan use to try to tempt Jesus to worship him?

3. Second Corinthians 11:14 tells us that "Satan himself masquerades as an angel of light." In your own words, what does *masquerade* mean?

4. Do you see a pattern in the way Satan works? What does he call into doubt when he interacts with us?

As you can see in this brief survey of Scripture, Satan's primary work is to cast doubt on God's *intentions* and attack the core of our *identity*. Titus 3:3 illustrates the results of Satan's work when our primary relationship with God is broken:

> *At one time we too were foolish, disobedient, deceived and enslaved by all kinds of passions and pleasures. We lived in malice and envy, being hated and hating one another.*

5. What is the result of being "enslaved"?

Application

Thomas Watson said, "Till sin be bitter, Christ cannot be sweet."[2]

Close your time with prayer. Maybe today you are recognizing for the first time that your struggles are much deeper than what you see on the surface. Grave problems require a glorious solution—and that is what we have in Christ!

Now is also a great time to pray specifically about those areas where you've recognized that you are harboring doubt about God's intentions and your identity.

This closing prayer is based on Romans 8:35-39:

Jesus Christ, You've promised that nothing can ever separate us from Your love. Whether we are in trouble, or struggling, or in need, or in danger, or even being threatened with death—no, despite all these things, overwhelming victory is ours through You, Jesus, because You love us.

So we are convinced that nothing can ever separate us from Your love! Neither death nor life, neither angels nor demons, neither our fears for today nor our worries about tomorrow—not even the powers of hell can separate us from Your love! No power in the sky above or in the earth below— indeed, nothing in all creation will ever be able to separate us from Your love!

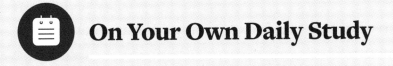

On Your Own Daily Study

THIS SESSION'S RECOMMENDED READING:
Chapters 3 and 4 in **The Struggle Is Real**

This is an inside-out week. We are taking the beliefs that have been on the inside and bringing them out into the light, turning them over in the presence of God's promises and examining where we may be experiencing the results of brokenness. Eek! That may sound a little heavy, but making the choice to face our reality—even the hard reality—leads to growth. Let's do it together!

Day 1
Life in the Word

RECOMMENDED BIBLE READING:
Deuteronomy 8:1-6

Today we start with a foundational truth that will guide the rest of our journey inward: *The Bible is the ultimate source of reality for living.*

Without an anchor for what's true and what isn't, we will find ourselves adrift on the whims and winds of our world. Without a foundation, whatever we build is bound to crumble when the storms come. Making the willful choice to believe the Bible and view it as our first point of reality allows us to actually examine what's true and what's not true in our stories.

Perhaps you've never even wondered whether the Scriptures are credible—or you have, but you aren't sure why you should believe they can be trusted. Let's take a look at what the Bible actually promises about itself.

Read the following verses closely to explore the benefits of God's Word. Highlight or underline any descriptors of God's Word. (The word *precept* means "a guiding principle or rule," and in this case, is used interchangeably with God's Word.)

Psalm 19:8

The precepts of the LORD are right, giving joy to the heart. The commands of the LORD are radiant, giving light to the eyes.

Psalm 111:7-10

The works of his hands are faithful and just; all his precepts are trustworthy. They are established for ever and ever, enacted in faithfulness and uprightness. He provided redemption for his people; he ordained his covenant forever—holy and awesome is his name. The fear of the LORD is the beginning of wisdom; all who follow his precepts have good understanding. To him belongs eternal praise.

Proverbs 30:5

Every word of God is flawless; he is a shield to those who take refuge in him.

Hebrews 4:12

The word of God is alive and active. Sharper than any double-edged sword, it penetrates even to dividing soul and spirit, joints and marrow; it judges the thoughts and attitudes of the heart.

1. Based on what you discovered in these passages, list some of the characteristics of God's Word:

2. List what God's Word *does*:

3. Finally, consider this final promise about the life-giving nature of Scripture:

Matthew 4:4

Jesus answered, "It is written: 'Man shall not live on bread alone, but on every word that comes from the mouth of God.'"

Recognize this verse from our group time? It is Jesus' response to the temptation of Satan. If Jesus Christ—the perfect, sinless Son of God—relied on Scripture to return Him to the truth, shouldn't we? Jesus is actually quoting from Deuteronomy 8:3, Moses' final words of encouragement to God's chosen people.

4. Read Deuteronomy 8:1-6. God communicated with the Israelites through their leader, Moses. Today the primary way He speaks to His people is through His Word. What does this passage tell us about how we are to respond to His message?

Day 2
The Promise of Hope

RECOMMENDED BIBLE READING:
Psalm 130

Let's take a look back at statements 4 through 6 in the Good Life Inventory (see page 8) that you completed in session 1.

+ I regularly and sincerely ask for forgiveness from my family, friends, and coworkers.

+ I respect my own heart, body, and soul as something to be cherished.

+ I treat conflicting patterns of thinking and behaving in myself with gentleness.

Pay attention to your thoughts, feelings, and actions for the rest of the week. As you do, consider how true these statements are about you.

Each of these declarations describes people of compassion—gentle, sincere, and respectful toward both their own story and others'. These responses are the fruit of a life grounded in the truth we find in God's Word about our humanity and His grace.

To find out what happens when we live into forgiveness, let's take a look at Psalm 130.

1. What are we able to do because of God's forgiveness in our life?

2. What is our job in this psalm? (Hint: look for the words *I*, *we*, *my*, and *Israel*.)

3. According to the psalmist, what does God do for us?

Thank God that He clarifies our roles when we relate to Him! Our responsibilities are to wait, to hope, and to call on Him. His are to forgive us fully, love us unfailingly, and redeem us completely. Amen!

Day 3
Extraordinary Value

RECOMMENDED BIBLE READING:
John 15:9-17

Today look again at statement 5 in the Good Life Inventory to consider what happens when we live in the intersection of confidence and humility:

> + I respect my own heart, body, and soul as something to be cherished.

1. To cherish means "to protect and care for" or "to hold (something) dear."[3] What is an object that you cherish? Why do you cherish it?

2. How would you feel if that object were somehow lost or damaged?

With those thoughts in mind, let's turn our attention to what God's Word says about His attention toward us as people to be cherished. These words may be familiar—so familiar that we tend to gloss over them without truly taking them in. In addition, as we become more honest with ourselves, we become painfully aware of areas of weakness and sin. As a result, we are less likely to treat ourselves as valuable.

Yet the glorious truth is that God already knows all of those unlovely things about you and loves you as you are. He delights in you and finds you so valuable that He provided a way for you to know His love and to be made whole in His presence. This is the good news of Jesus Christ.

3. Read the following Scriptures. If you struggle to believe you are cherished and valuable, ask God to help you believe that these promises are for you. Underline any words or phrases that stick out to you as you read:

Luke 12:6-7, 32, NLT

What is the price of five sparrows—two copper coins? Yet God does not forget a single one of them. And the very hairs on your head are all numbered. . . . So don't be afraid, little flock. For it gives your Father great happiness to give you the Kingdom.

Romans 5:8, NLT

God showed his great love for us by sending Christ to die for us while we were still sinners.

Ephesians 2:10, NLT

We are God's masterpiece. He has created us anew in Christ Jesus, so we can do the good things he planned for us long ago.

In his book *Ruthless Trust*, Brennan Manning writes, "Wrong thinking about God and people often begins with a debased image of ourselves."[4]

Consider that quote as you read the words or phrases you underlined above. Spend a few moments in God's presence, letting yourself believe that He regards you this way. In doing so, you are trusting God to transform you in His love.

Day 4
An Inner Grace

RECOMMENDED BIBLE READING:
Romans 8

Let's take a moment to look more closely at statement 6 in the Good Life Inventory:

> **+ I treat conflicting patterns of thinking and behaving in myself with gentleness.**

1. If gentleness is not your normal response to your own shortcomings, how do you respond (frustration, blame, denial, judgment, shame)?

2. Read Romans 7:15–8:2. How does Paul handle the disparity between what he says and what he does?

3. What is Paul's saving grace? (7:25)

4. Romans 8:1 says, "Therefore, there is no
   condemnation for those who are in Christ Jesus."
   The "therefore" connects this verse with the previous
   passage in chapter 7. Does connecting these two ideas
   change your perspective on the power of the "no
   condemnation" idea?

Friends, the apostle Paul penned the promise of Romans 8:1,
not as a victor who had overcome all of his struggles, but as
a fellow struggler who continued to live with the disorder of
sin. It is out of that place of struggle that the joy and power of
Romans 8 flows. As you go about your day, pay attention to
your inner dialogue. Make a choice to treat your own inner
disorder with gentleness, not condemnation.

Day 5
A Seeking God

RECOMMENDED BIBLE READING:
Proverbs 19:8, 20-23

This week's focus has been on gaining an increased aware-ness of your inner world. Perhaps this has been a real struggle because when you look inward, you don't like what you see!

We are often more selfish, more fearful, and far less lov-ing and kind than we want to admit. It is easier to pretend this reality doesn't exist, but the inner struggle between who we are and who we want to be won't go away on its own. To ignore it might feel easier, but to do so dilutes the power of grace in the places where we need it the most!

Romans 2:4 tells us, "God's kindness is intended to lead you to repentance."

It is the kindness of God that shows you who you really are. Repentance isn't about rattling off a list of your poor behaviors and then crawling to God's feet seeking mercy because of all the ways you don't measure up. Repentance is about changing your heart and mind. And your mind-set must change from the mistaken belief that you can mend your brokenness to an understanding that *you cannot fix yourself.*

1. Read Psalm 139. What does this tell you about God's heart toward you?

2. The psalmist David describes the Lord as his loving and all-knowing Creator, his constant source of strength and guidance. David closes the psalm this way:

   Search me, God, and know my heart;
   *   test me and know my anxious thoughts.*
   See if there is any offensive way in me,
   *   and lead me in the way everlasting.*

   Turn the passage above into a prayer, inviting God to examine your heart and mind. Then spend a few minutes asking God to bring to mind those places in your life where you've tried to fix yourself. Imagine submitting yourself to a soul scan in which you allow God to bring to mind any places that you've hidden from His loving gaze. Record your impressions below.

Why do the hard inner work of accepting who you really are? One direct result of a growing compassion for your own brokenness is a growing compassion for others. Jesus told us to love our neighbors as ourselves—and truly, when we love ourselves with the love God has for us, we will love our neighbor as well. Proverbs 19:8 says, "The one who gets wisdom loves life." When we surrender to God's way and wisdom, we discover an expansive, abundant love that completely rewrites our story.

A seeking prayer:

Good Father, it is out of Your love that You gently lead me to the truth of myself. Help me not to shy away, blame, cower, or hide from the truth. Give me the faith to believe that there is no condemnation in Jesus Christ, and that it is Your pleasure when I come to You fully transparent, in the promise of Your full love. Amen.

Session Three

Freedom in the Struggle

The freedom cycle always stretches our hearts—
sometimes painfully, sometimes gloriously—into the
new story that God invites us to write with Him.

The Struggle Is Real, chapter 6, page 133

Freedom—we all want it, but no one quite knows where to find it, what it feels like on an everyday basis, and how we can possibly live it out completely. This week, we discover that freedom is what we were made for—but it takes work to believe it! Let's do that work together as we learn how—at just the right time—Jesus has set us free.

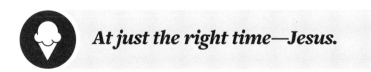 *At just the right time—Jesus.*

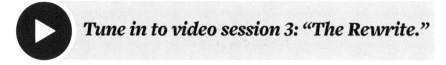

Tune in to video session 3: "The Rewrite."

Video Notes

"Everything that we have—right thinking and right living, a clean slate and a fresh start—comes from God by way of Jesus Christ" (1 Corinthians 1:30, MSG).

Without Christ, there is no real freedom.

The wisdom of Christ transforms the way we understand ourselves.

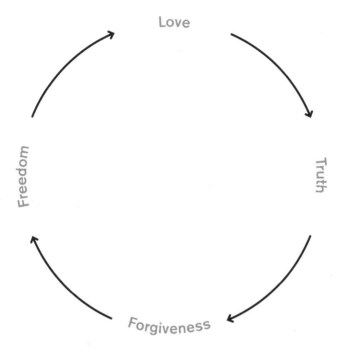

AJ's Story

"Of course on the outside I would be nice or kind toward people, [but] it was definitely all out of this: 'I have to do that, I have to be like that, in order to be a good Christian.'"

 **Reflection**

1. Can you relate to AJ's story? Have you ever misinterpreted God's character and intentions?

2. When it comes to the freedom cycle, where are you most comfortable with God's character? What is a stretch for you?

 **In the Word**

The ultimate rewrite—the way we understand our past and live into the future—comes when we understand Christ's work in our lives.

1. Let's turn to John 8:2-11, a passage that shows Jesus' freedom nature in full color. Read the story aloud and try to imagine what it must have felt like to be in the crowd that day.

2. In this passage, what are the actions of the woman?

3. What are the actions of Jesus?

You are right if you noticed that the woman does nothing—or at least nothing that's recorded! I imagine she's terrified—but Scripture says nothing about her feeling contrite, repentant, or ashamed. We don't know if she even regrets her sin. *Scripture speaks loudly when it says nothing at all.* It's important to note that there is not one part of this interaction that has to do with her character—0 percent. She brings no words or actions to the table.

Now let's look to the actions of Jesus. In contrast to the woman, what does Jesus do? Journal what Jesus might have been intending to communicate in the way He interacts with the religious leaders, the crowd, and the woman.

4. How does the freedom cycle relate to the story of the woman in John 8?

Application

Think about a place in your life where you tend to harbor shame. Have you ever felt condemned (by your own judgment, by others, by your actions)? Is there a moment in your story that needs to be rewritten in light of Christ's call to set you free? Share here about one of those places, and if you are in a group, pray for one another, that you might experience Jesus saying in love, "Neither do I condemn you."

On Your Own Daily Study

THIS SESSION'S RECOMMENDED READING:
Chapters 5 and 6 in The Struggle Is Real

Last week we examined the gravity of our brokenness and considered how serious problems require a serious solution! This week we are shifting our focus to what God has done for us through Jesus and how that changes everything about the way we understand our story.

Day 1
The Redeemed Story, Part 1

RECOMMENDED BIBLE READING:
Psalm 107:1-16

The fruit of our life in Christ is illustrated by the following two statements from our Good Life Inventory:

+ I feel total freedom from my past hurts and regrets.

+ I experience joy on a daily basis.

God desires each of us to know the glorious freedom of being identified as His children. But the ramifications of sin mean that each of us also must engage in an intentional journey to live in that freedom. Psalm 107 is a call to praise for the great works of God in our lives, told through a series of story themes. Each of these themes invites us to consider how God has worked to rescue, heal, redeem, and save us, as evident in the story of our own lives.

Let's orient ourselves to the purpose of this psalm, which begins like this:

> *Give thanks to the LORD, for he is good;*
> *his love endures forever.*

1. Read Psalm 107:2 and then write down the command God gives in this verse:

> *Let the redeemed of the LORD tell their story—*
> *those he redeemed from the hand of the foe,*

2. The closing verse of Psalm 107 says:

> *Let the one who is wise heed these things*
> *And ponder the loving deeds of the LORD.*

Why do you think God calls us to both *tell* our story and *remember* our story?

3. Read Psalm 107:4-9. This passage introduces the first story theme of being lost and found. What words or phrases in these verses resonate with you?

4. Now read Psalm 107:10-16. The second story theme is that of being bound and set free. Have you experienced the consequences of poor behavior in your life? If so, how?

5. Turn to Romans 6:16. What have you felt enslaved to in the past? Is there anything that feels enslaving in your life right now?

As you go about your day, pay attention to experiences that may trigger the "lost" or "bound" story theme in your life. Remind your soul that your true reality is that you've been found and freed in Christ.

Day 2

The Redeemed Story, Part 2

RECOMMENDED BIBLE READING:
Psalm 107:17-38

Today we will examine two more story themes found in Psalm 107. We can't know where we are going if we don't know where we are coming from! This psalm gives us the opportunity to engage with where we've been when living outside of Christ's love.

1. Read Psalm 107:17-22. This passage centers on the theme of affliction—becoming "fools" because of our actions, whether unintentionally or intentionally. Either way, they have created patterns of pain and suffering in our lives. What did God use to bring healing to those trapped in this story theme (see verse 20)?

2. Here we see an allusion to Christ. It is Jesus who offers to heal our sickness (see Mark 2:17). It is Jesus who has overcome the power of the grave (see 1 Corinthians

15:55-57)! In light of your own story, what hope do you find in these passages?

3. Now read Psalm 107:23-30. While the first three story themes focused on the inner storms of being lost, bound, or afflicted, this final story theme focuses on the outer storm of becoming overwhelmed by circumstances outside your control. Have you ever looked back and thought that God might have brought an intentional storm into your life to draw you toward Him? If so, describe that experience.

4. Let the redeemed of the Lord tell their story! In Psalm 107, we find four story themes that serve as examples of what our rescued and redeemed story looks like. If you were to write your own story in a similar way, what would you say? For instance:

I was living for the god of approval and achievement, and as a result, my inner world was crumbling under the pressure. I cried out to God and discovered the promise of Romans 8 in His Word, realizing for the first time that not even I could separate myself from Christ's love. In that moment, I experienced freedom from the burden of being perfect and pleasing the world.

Now it's your turn. To begin the process, fill in the blanks below:

I was _____and the results were _____.

I cried out to God by _____.

God _____ me.

If you'd like, take these notes and expand them into a paragraph that explains more specifically how Christ has been redeeming your story.

Day 3
The Freedom Cycle

RECOMMENDED BIBLE READING:
Psalm 103:1-22

The way we become people of freedom is by living into our redeemed story. As we get a taste of that freedom, we want it all the more. Because of God's mercy, we can develop a growing sense of the freedom we have in Christ throughout our lives! So if that's the case, how do we take our redeemed story and keep living into that freedom? How do we know we are really free? Let's revisit the freedom cycle and make it personal for today.

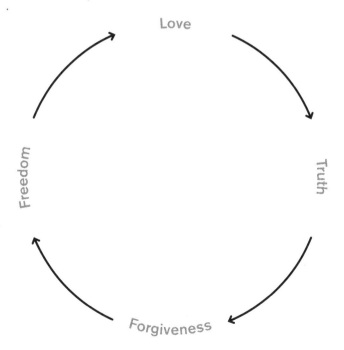

We cannot know God in pieces. His essence can be fully known only if we embrace all of His character. Just as we cannot separate people's minds from their hearts, we cannot separate the fundamentals of God when we are in a relationship with Him.

If you know only one aspect of God's character, you will miss out on the fullness of who He is. Let's grasp the greatness of who He is today! I invite you to read and then record some important promises about His nature below. Use this time of reflection and writing to let these truths sink deeply into your heart.

God's Love
Zephaniah 3:17

The fruit of knowing God's love is security in your inner world and the courage to be vulnerable.

Truth
Psalm 25:5

Psalm 145:18

The fruit of knowing truth is a deep desire for wholeness combined with an awareness of your inability to fix yourself.

Forgiveness
Matthew 26:28

Acts 13:38

The fruit of living in forgiveness is experiencing inner healing and wholeness.

Freedom
2 Corinthians 3:17

The fruit of living in freedom is an expanded sense of peace and joy in your life.

As you understand God's love, truth, forgiveness, and freedom, you begin to mature. Maturity in Christ involves a growing dependence on His presence and guidance, and a growing compassion and love for who and what God cares about. You aren't just someone who makes wise choices; you become wise yourself. That is the work of the Holy Spirit in you, pointing you to Christ and drawing you near to the Father. Truly, you become free!

Freedom Derailers

RECOMMENDED BIBLE READING:
Galatians 5:1, 7-8

Now that we've spent time with the freedom cycle, let's talk about some of the big (and little) ways we can derail off the cycle. Check out this description from *The Struggle Is Real* (page 128):

> It's often easier to diagnose what's going on in our hearts by what's *not* going right than by what is. And when it comes to the freedom cycle, there are places where we derail all the time. If we aren't experiencing all of God's character, then we quickly veer off. If we know God's love but we don't know His truth, that's a problem. If we know His forgiveness but don't move toward freedom, that's a problem. There is not one element in the cycle that we can bypass and still know the fullness of God, or His essence. Just as you can't be fully known by someone who refuses to recognize important elements in your personality, so we can't know God in His fullness if we don't acknowledge all aspects of His being. And freedom derailers are a sign that we are missing out on an aspect of God's goodness. Think of these derailers as off-ramps on the freedom cycle, where instead of embracing the next aspect of God, we accidentally head a different way.

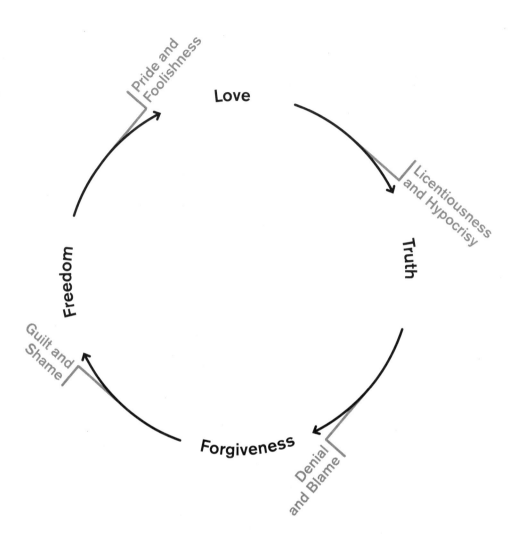

Love derailers: If you embrace God's love but don't let it lead you to rigorous truth about your broken story and the broken-storied people around you, you will off-ramp into licentiousness and hypocrisy. God's love without God's truth will give you a distorted view of yourself and others.

Truth derailers: If you reckon with the truth but don't desire forgiveness and extend it to others, you will off-ramp into denying who you really are. "People who conceal their sins will not prosper, but if they confess and turn from them, they will receive mercy" (Proverbs 28:13, NLT). Your off-ramp will be denial or blame.

Forgiveness derailers: If you experience forgiveness but do not accept the freedom that comes with it, your off-ramp will lead you into guilt and shame. You will stay in a perpetual cycle of whipping yourself with your former sins—always beaten, never victorious.

Freedom derailers: If you live in God's freedom but don't allow His love to shape your freedom, you will detour into pride and foolishness. You will use His freedom to justify your own actions, rather than letting that freedom lead you into deeper, sacrificial love.

Spend a few moments with these definitions. Think back to a time recently when you derailed in one of these ways. What do you think caused you to derail? *(Remember: The purpose of this exercise is not to shame or condemn yourself, but to discover the places where you need to lean in to aspects of God's nature. Ask God to reveal Himself in the places that are less known to you.)*

Day 5
Living Redeemed

RECOMMENDED BIBLE READING:
Psalm 28

This week we've done a deep dive into our redeemed story.

One of the greatest results of understanding the way God has redeemed our story is that it creates in us a desire to worship God. When we realize His majesty and power in light of our frailty, our natural response is gratitude and worship. As you review what you've learned this week about your own story and God's character, spend some time thanking God for the specific ways He's redeemed your life:

Take a look at the definition of the word *redeemed*:

Redeem:
to free from what **distresses** or harms: as
a: to **free from captivity** by payment of ransom
b: to **extricate** from or help to overcome something detrimental
c: to **release** from blame or debt: clear
d: to **free from the consequences** of sin[5]

As you consider God's work within your story, which aspect of this definition resonates most with you—either because you see God at work in this way or because you would like to see Him move this way in your life? Explain.

Praise God, who redeems our stories and sets us free to a life of joy and peace in Him! We truly become people who can answer the statements from the Good Life Inventory below with a resounding *yes*:

+ I feel total freedom from my past hurts and regrets.

+ I experience joy on a daily basis.

Let's paraphrase part of Psalm 28 to close in prayer this week:

Lord, You are my strength and my shield. My heart trusts in You, and You are a helper to me. My heart leaps for joy because of Your love, and I want to sing Your praises! Lord, I sing You my freedom song because You are worthy of my worship—and it's all because of Jesus. Thank You, Father! Amen.

Foundations

Though no one escapes the struggle, we all have a choice
to make about how the struggle writes the story.

The Struggle Is Real, chapter 8, page 180

We often use the word *integrity* to describe a person's character, but it's also a word used to describe sound structures. When a building's foundation is strong, it has integrity. A foundation with integrity is whole and undivided. Likewise, to be a person of integrity, our foundation must be whole and undivided. This week, we explore our foundations and then invite God to repair the cracks and shore up weaknesses that require His touch. Let's begin the renovation work!

The past impacts but does not define my future.

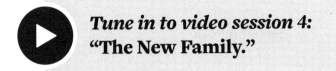

Tune in to video session 4:
"The New Family."

Video Notes

Your freedom has a purpose.

Dysfunction is contagious.

When it comes to understanding ourselves, our past impacts—but doesn't have to direct—our future.

Jon's Story

"If I can give them a healthy sense of identity, a healthy sense of family, and a healthy sense of heritage, that's what I want to pass down to my children. . . . It's about a sense of

freedom and joy about who they are—as blessed and loved
children adopted by our Lord to be with Him forever."

 ## Reflection

1. On a scale of 1 to 10, how spiritually purposeful does
   your everyday life feel?

2. As you listened to Jon's story, did you recognize any
   aspects of yourself that you've tried to hide?

3. What does "identity in Christ" mean to you? How does
   that play out in everyday life?

4. Do you ever feel like you are living a life "on repeat" from your past? What aspects of your life (positive or negative) seem to repeat themselves?

 **In the Word**

In order to hear the truth of our new story, we need to know our heavenly Author's voice. Author Dallas Willard says, "Only our *communion* with God provides the appropriate context for *communications* between us and him."[6] In other words, when we define our relationship with God, we understand how to engage in conversation. I converse differently with my child as opposed to my boss. I share differently with my best friend as opposed to my mailman.

1. Let's look at how Jesus explains His communication with us. Here are several key phrases from John 10. Look for imagery within these phrases, and take note of what thoughts and feelings come to mind.

Verse 9

I am the gate; whoever enters through me will be saved. They will come in and go out, and find pasture.

Verse 10

The thief comes only to steal and kill and destroy; I have come that they may have life, and have it to the full.

Verse 11

I am the good shepherd. The good shepherd lays down his life for the sheep.

Verse 14

I am the good shepherd; I know my sheep and my sheep know me—just as the Father knows me and I know the Father—and I lay down my life for the sheep.

Verse 27

My sheep listen to my voice; I know them, and they follow me.

THE STRUGGLE IS REAL PARTICIPANT'S GUIDE

Verse 28

I give them eternal life, and they shall never perish; no one will snatch them out of my hand.

Verses 29 and 30

My Father, who has given them to me, is greater than all; no one can snatch them out of my Father's hand. I and the Father are one.

2. One of the ways Jesus defines our relationship with God is by calling Him Father. How does your relationship with your earthly father color your understanding of God as Father?

3. Take a moment to write down what you desire to hear from your heavenly Father. What might God speak to your heart that would allow you to lean into your new and free story?

4. Now let's look at a few passages that help us know *how* we can expect to hear from God. Turn to Habakkuk 2:14. What aspects of creation reveal the nature of God to you?

5. Next read 2 Timothy 3:16. How have you experienced God's Word being useful in your life? Can you think of a specific example from the past week?

6. Finally, turn to John 16:13. What is the role of the Holy Spirit in helping us hear from God?

Application

The idea of hearing from God can feel as if it's reserved for the superspiritual or mystics among us. But Scripture makes it clear that God speaks—drawing us into worship, into truth, and into the good works "which God prepared in advance for us to do" (Ephesians 2:10). He speaks to us through His creation, through other believers, and through His Word. Close your time together by spending a few minutes in silence, asking for God's leading, and then jot down any specific insights for yourself or, if you are in a group, any encouragement for others that comes to mind.

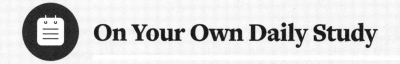

On Your Own Daily Study

THIS WEEK'S RECOMMENDED READING:
***Chapters 7 and 8 in* The Struggle Is Real**

This week, we move into the work of living into our new and true story. In order to do this, we need to know how to hear from God. We also need to take a look back at our life so that we can move forward with freedom. In the end, we want to be able to live out these positive statements from our Good Life Inventory:

+ **I have a clear sense of purpose in my life.**

+ **I have experienced deep compassion for someone who has hurt me.**

Day 1
Holistic Living

RECOMMENDED BIBLE READING:
Mark 12:28-34

Recently, I had a few minutes of reflection with a friend. We lamented a season of life and a culture that seem to demand more from us than we could ever give. The "shoulds" are overwhelming. We should work out every day, spend time in the Word, fit in quality conversation with our children, cook nutritious meals, show up with excellence at work, and somehow also stay up on the latest trends. We should minimize technology and maximize creativity, not only for ourselves but for all the people we are responsible for. It's as if we are expected to live fifty hours in a twenty-four-hour day—exhausting and impossible! Do you ever feel like the spiritual life is just as taxing? Let's look together at the incredible, impossible, and freeing call of life in Christ.

1. Read Matthew 22:37-39. What requires our "all"?

2. The word *all* in the Greek is *holos*, which is the root for our word *holistic*.[7] When you think of the idea of loving God holistically, how does that relate to painful circumstances or relationships from your past or present?

3. Turn to Galatians 5:13 and record the words and phrases that stand out to you:

4. According to this verse, what does freedom do in
   your life?

If what God is asking for in the greatest commandments
seems impossible, take heart! That's a good place to be.
Loving God holistically and using our freedom to love others
is *supposed* to feel impossible—and without the indwelling
power of Christ, equipping you for every good work, it is.

Close your time by bringing to mind any relationships
and memories from your past and fears from your present
that need God's healing touch. Don't try to fix them or clean
them up. Just imagine bringing them to the throne of grace
and leaving them in God's hands for His purposes.

Day 2
Why It's Worth It

RECOMMENDED BIBLE READING:
2 Corinthians 5:11-21

You might wonder why it's so important to reexamine your own story. Why would you ever want to remember hurtful relationships, painful circumstances, or unreconciled family relationships? As human beings, we tend to seek pleasure and avoid pain, so starting off your day with hard work may not appeal. But don't forget—*the struggle is the story.*

Also remember that when you can see what you are working for, it's sometimes easier to do the hard work. Read the following Scriptures and underline the phrases that tell us about our job on earth:

Ephesians 2:10

We are God's handiwork, created in Christ Jesus to do good works, which God prepared in advance for us to do.

2 Corinthians 5:18-21, NLT

All of this is a gift from God, who brought us back to himself through Christ. And God has given us this task of reconciling people to him. For God was in Christ, reconciling the world to himself, no longer

counting people's sins against them. And he gave
us this wonderful message of reconciliation. So we are
Christ's ambassadors; God is making his appeal through
us. We speak for Christ when we plead, "Come back to
God!" For God made Christ, who never sinned, to be
the offering for our sin, so that we could be made right
with God through Christ.

It is clear that we have been given a mandate, and we won't experience the fullness of Christ unless we take part in the work He gives us to do. Your "work" might look like faithful living in your family, diligent service in your workplace, or persevering prayer for a loved one's salvation. The question is never *if* you have work to do. It's what you will do with the work God has given you.

One important point—there is a huge difference between the works that come through faith and freedom, and the work you and I do to try to prove that we are worthy or good. The results can look exactly the same externally—we may say and do all the right things—but the internal setting of our hearts is what matters.

When we work for Christ, we aren't working *toward* Christ; we are working *in* Christ. The work of our salvation has been done on the cross. It is completely finished. The work of our salvation rests fully in Christ. Now God calls us to live into that freedom story and join God in His work.

To close today's daily work, turn to Philippians 3:16 and write down the mandate:

We look back so that we might move forward in freedom! We present the painful places in our soul to God so that He might heal and redeem them and we can live out what we have already attained. Go in that strength today.

Day 3
Search Me, Know Me

RECOMMENDED BIBLE READING:
Romans 12:1-2

Author David Benner says, "If we find our true self we find God, and if we find God, we find our most authentic self."[8] Finding our true self is not easy. We are complex individuals who go to great lengths to hide the less desirable parts of ourselves. However, self-examination is never enough; rather, we join with the psalmist to say, "Search me, God, and know my heart" (Psalm 139:23). Just as a skilled doctor can explain the illness behind your symptoms, Jesus, our Great Physician, can explain the motives behind our actions.

All of us have patterns of sin in our life, ways of thinking, feeling, and acting that work independently of our identity in Christ. Today we will look at the origins of some of those patterns, which often flow out of our childhood experiences.

Let's think of one positive and one negative experience to explore together. Generally, a memory from your childhood (age five to twelve) is a good place to start. It doesn't need to be a big moment—just let a memory come to mind.

Here's an example of how to use the chart below: Let's say I have a positive memory of winning a soccer game when I was a kid. I might write in the first space under "Positive Memory": "Winning made me feel worthy, successful, and joyful. It taught me that I love to win. I still live this out when I choose to compete instead of cooperate at work."

In this particular example, a positive memory has still created a negative sin pattern.

To finish the example, I might fill in the last box: "The truth is, winning is great but winning isn't everything. I want to watch for that tendency in me this week."

Now it's your turn. Once one positive and one negative memory come to mind, fill in each space in the chart.

Positive Memory	Negative Memory
This memory makes me feel:	This memory makes me feel:
It taught me that:	It taught me that:
I still live this out when:	I still live this out when:
The truth is:	The truth is:

Inviting God's loving and healing eyes into our memories allows the Spirit of God to "lead us into all truth" (John 16:13). We all live out of story lines that no longer need to define us. We can make a choice to live into a full and free life, but it's going to take work! Praise God, who meets us in the memories and provides gentle correction toward the truth, so that we may be truly free.

Day 4
The Power of Self-Examination

RECOMMENDED BIBLE READING:
Psalm 139

Just as memories have the power to obscure the truth of our freedom in Christ, the dynamic between our temperament (the way we are wired) and our environment (the home we grew up in) can also create sin patterns that distort the truth.

Many personality inventories can provide language to help you understand and appreciate the way you experience the world. After taking an assessment, many people report new depths of understanding themselves—both strengths and weaknesses, as well as the way they process the world and interact with others.

A word of wisdom, though: Personality inventories are not the inspired Word of God! They aren't an oracle for your future or a diagnosis of your past. Inventories only provide a springboard for self-examination and new words for your experiences. As we heard in Erin's story, an inventory cannot and should not define you—God does that. However, such resources can lead to greater self-understanding.

Online options include

Myers-Briggs Personality Inventory: 16personalities.com
Enneagram Inventory: exploreyourtype.com
DISC: discpersonalitytesting.com

StrengthsFinder (paid test): several options at
Gallupstrengthscenter.com

Each of these options has a myriad of follow-up tools
(many accessible online) that can facilitate further discussion.
Consider working with your group to choose one inventory
to dive into and explore together.

Another great way to explore your temperament is
through the eyes of those who knew you growing up. If you
have healthy family relationships, you can ask your parents
or extended family about some of the patterns they have
observed in you, using the questions below. If not, you might
be able to think back by exploring any of the following questions. The purpose of this exercise is to allow you to fill out
your story—who you've been, what you've believed, and
what's actually true about you.

1. Were you a rule keeper, rule bender, or rule breaker?
   Was your behavior similar or different depending on
   the environment (school, home, social events)?

2. How did you handle conflict in your family?

3. How were emotions (positive and negative) treated in your family?

4. What kind of student were you? What would a teacher have said about you?

5. What is your place in your family's birth order? Do you think you have the stereotypical tendencies associated with the oldest (leader), middle (peacekeeper), or youngest child (free spirit)?

6. As a child, did you prefer to be with others or to be alone? Were you given the freedom to be yourself?

7. As a child, how did you express creativity (building, acting, singing, role-playing, exploring, etc.)? Was that celebrated or frowned upon?

8. How do you feel similar to your ten-year-old self? How do you feel different?

9. If you could go back to your teenage self, what would you want to tell him or her?

This kind of exploration takes time, but it's worth the work. Remember, God already knows your true self. He's not scared, surprised, or disgusted by who you really are. He delights in you and desires for you to know the freedom of knowing Him and knowing yourself through Him. The core question we are asking is, Who have I been, and who is God making me to be? Trust the process.

Day 5
Consider the Creator

RECOMMENDED BIBLE READING:
Psalm 19:1-2

Today's exercise involves getting your eyes off the page and into the skies. Spend ten minutes today outside, whether during the day or at night. If daytime, raise your eyes to the sky for several moments. Take deep breaths and ask God to "pour forth His speech" through His creation. Imagine holding up whatever burden you've carried this week and releasing it to His care.

If it's nighttime, raise your eyes to the stars. What can you discover about the way the heavens "reveal knowledge" that you can apply to your life today?

After spending a few minutes simply taking in the creation, write about what you experienced when you studied the skies.

If we were honest, I think many of us would admit that we wish God would reveal Himself in a very narrow kind of way. We might imagine hearing an audible voice, seeing a message written in the sky, or receiving a Holy Spirit signal through a license plate. But God has made it clear that His entire creation is speaking to us!

Praise God, who has written a story in the heavens and earth, who has written a story through His Word, and who continues to write Himself into your story—past, present, and future!

Let's close our discovery week with prayer together:

Good Father, I admit that I want to know the end of this story. Exploring who I've been and who I'm becoming can be an uncomfortable process. I wonder if You are going to finish what You've started in me. But I believe in Your promises—that I am Your handiwork, and that You will complete the good work You have begun. Father, I want my story to be written by You—Your truth, Your love, Your freedom. Help me to understand my life through Your eyes. Amen.

The Rewrite

Our inner speech shapes our inner world,
impacting our attitudes, behaviors, and
engagement with the world outside of our heads.

The Struggle Is Real, chapter 9, page 193

This week, we turn our attention to the work of rewriting our story in light of God's wisdom. If you've ever overheard children talking to themselves, you know the incredible capacity we have for inner speech. We speak words to ourselves that shape our reality, and when our reality is reshaped by God, we must do the work of listening, understanding, and rewriting our inner speech to represent the truth of our love, worth, freedom, and identity in Christ. As Ralph Waldo Emerson said, "Speech is power—speech is to persuade, to convert, to compel."[9] Let's look at how we begin the process of rewriting our lives with wisdom.

 Wisdom takes work—and it's worth it.

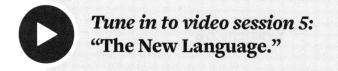

Tune in to video session 5: "The New Language."

Video Notes

"Words make worlds." (Krista Tippett)

The tongue has the power of life and death (Proverbs 18:21).

The fruit of the Spirit is manifest through our words: with God, ourselves, and others.

Alli's Story

"I had to stop speaking to myself in a way of hate and in a way of worthlessness. . . . I had to stop speaking to myself

so harshly and without grace—because I realized so much negativity in my head was affecting everything in my life."

 **Reflection**

1. What are the first three words that come to mind to describe yourself? (Be honest!)

2. Do you have an inner critic? What does he/she sound like?

3. Alli spoke about making a choice to rewrite her inner language. Do you have intentional ways of hearing the truth? What works for you?

4. When it comes to bearing the fruit of the Spirit through your words, where do you need the most help—in the way you speak with God, with yourself, or with others?

In the Word

Turn to Luke 6. As we read this practical teaching from Jesus on wise living, remember that the motive behind all commands is love. In his brilliant simplicity, Jesus gives us analogies that illustrate what love is and how love operates. Each of these passages provides a new interpretation for our own story lines.

1. Read Luke 6:41-42. Jesus paints a ridiculous and accurate picture of humanity when he speaks of the plank and the speck. It has been said that we loathe in others what we actually see in ourselves. What is the proper order of action in this passage?

Some may read this passage and immediately surmise that we should never engage truth with others. Maybe it feels easier to just leave your brother's speck and your plank intact! But that's not Jesus' command here. Rather, he calls us to rigorous self-examination and compassionate and gentle engagement in relationships.

2. Now read Luke 6:43-45 and Matthew 15:16-20. Jesus moves his analogy from the eye to the mouth. Look back at Matthew 15:8. What principle is Jesus teaching through these passages?

3. Why is it easier to focus on our actions than on our hearts?

4. Finally, read Luke 6:46-49. What does it mean for you to put Jesus' words into practice?

Application

The great preacher Charles Spurgeon said the following about this passage in Luke about the wise and foolish builders: "The common temptation is, instead of really repenting, to *talk about* repentance, instead of heartily believing, to *say*, 'I believe,' without believing, instead of truly loving, to talk of love, without loving, instead of coming to Christ, to speak about coming to Christ, and profess to come to Christ, and yet not to come at all."[10]

> Spurgeon's quote speaks of the practices that build a foundation of faith: repentance, belief, love, and seeking to be with Christ. What foundation do you need to build, rebuild, or strengthen this week?

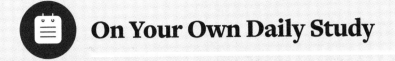 # On Your Own Daily Study

THIS WEEK'S RECOMMENDED READING:
Chapter 9 in **The Struggle Is Real**

This week, we continue with the work of living into our new and true story, and now we get down to the nitty-gritty of change. Perhaps you've lived with the assumption that because spiritual work is internal and invisible, it happens without intention. But the reality is, all work is work. And the work of believing your new story takes willful, active, repeated choices.

If you needed to strengthen a muscle in your body, you would continually engage the muscle with force, breaking down the fibers so they could rebuild stronger. You cannot rebuild a muscle by watching someone else work out— watching a workout isn't working out! You cannot rebuild a life by continuing the same thought patterns and habits that you've always had.

Let's journey this week through the rewriting process.

Day 1

The Workout of the Mind

RECOMMENDED BIBLE READING:
2 Corinthians 3

The fruit of new living begins with changing our minds. But how exactly do we begin to change the way we think? Let's begin today by talking about how change happens in our minds.

1. Read Romans 12:1-2:

> I urge you, brothers and sisters, in view of God's mercy, to offer your bodies as a living sacrifice, holy and pleasing to God—this is your true and proper worship. Do not conform to the pattern of this world, but be transformed by the renewing of your mind. Then you will be able to test and approve what God's will is—his good, pleasing and perfect will.

As you read this passage a second time, circle all the action verbs related to what you must do to be transformed.

Note that the verb for *be transformed* is passive—meaning that the action is being done to the object. The active phrases are "offer your bodies," "do not conform," and "by the renewing of your mind." The result of these actions is the ability to "test and approve what God's will is."

Paul gives us clear action steps in this passage for how we will be transformed, able to know God's will:

a. *Give*: offer our bodies (our whole selves) in worship.
b. *Reject*: do not live in the patterns of the world (see day 5).
c. *Act*: actively renew your mind (see days 2 through 4).

Today let's start with step one: *give*.

There are two aspects of giving: what we want to give away and what we must give up.

When we've surrendered our lives to Jesus Christ, we give away our *rights*. This does not mean that we are no longer ourselves; rather, it means that we give away our right to define our own lives, to decide the way life should go, and to judge what's most important. We surrender our lives to the words of Christ. We decide that what He says is what matters, what He believes is what's important, and how He directs our lives will lead to the best lives.

2. Read Romans 12:1-2 again. Then in your own words, describe how giving yourself over to God in this way is your worship.

Surrendering to Christ may feel heavy and hard to you, and if so, there's pride or fear at work in your soul. As hard as it might be to admit, when we resist surrender, we aren't willing to trust our Lord. It might be because you have a rebellious part of your heart that wants to be in charge, independent of God. Or it might be because you are scared of God and what it will mean to commit to Him. Most likely, you feel a mixture of both. But God is gracious with us, slow to anger and rich in love. He is patient with us, not wanting anyone to perish but for everyone to come to the knowledge of the truth (see Psalm 103:8; 2 Peter 3:9). Remember—belief takes work.

Here's the really good news, though: When we surrender our lives to Jesus Christ, we also hand our burdens to Him. When we give Him everything, that includes our fears, our concerns, and our pain. We give up the confusion. We give up the worry. We give up the suffocating pressure to get it all right.

3. In the last question, you considered what it looks like to give yourself over to God. Now think about what you would like to willingly give up to God as your worship. What burdens are you holding on to that you would like to let go?

All of this is the practical outworking of Jesus' words: "If you cling to your life, you will lose it; but if you give up your life for me, you will find it" (Matthew 10:39, NLT).

On the other side of surrender is freedom. *The more honest you are about your need for rescue, the sweeter your freedom will be!*

Day 2
The Gift of Hope

RECOMMENDED BIBLE READING:
Psalm 16

There is a secret ingredient needed for mental transformation. Let's look at where we find that ingredient today:

Dr. Caroline Leaf, a cognitive neuroscientist, studies the impact of words in our brains, and consequently, our lives. She says, "Thoughts are real, physical things that occupy mental real estate. Moment by moment, every day, you are changing the structure of your brain through your thinking. When we *hope*, it is an activity of the mind that changes the structure of our brain in a positive and normal direction."[11]

Now read these verses about how we experience hope:

Psalm 25:5

Guide me in your truth and teach me, for you are God my Savior, and my hope is in you all day long.

Psalm 42:5

Why, my soul, are you downcast? Why so disturbed within me? Put your hope in God, for I will yet praise him, my Savior and my God.

Psalm 119:147

I rise before dawn and cry for help; I have put my hope in your word.

Psalm 147:11

The LORD delights in those who fear him, who put their hope in his unfailing love.

Lamentations 3:21-26

This I call to mind and therefore I have hope: Because of the LORD's great love we are not consumed, for his compassions never fail. They are new every morning; great is your faithfulness. I say to myself, "The LORD is my portion; therefore I will wait for him." The LORD is good to those whose hope is in him, to the one who seeks him; it is good to wait quietly for the salvation of the LORD.

1. Rewriting our relationship with God begins with knowing the hope that He offers us in daily life. Write down what you learn about hope based on the verses above:

   •

   •

   •

•

•

•

2. Based on what you've read in Scripture, what can you confidently ask God for today?

As we learned together in group time, we can talk all day about belief, but not actually believe. Hope is found in believing that God can rewrite your story from the inside out. Hope is found in creating new pathways in your mind that move you toward the truth of God's love and engagement with you today!

A closing prayer:

God, You have said that my hope can be in You all day long. Forgive me for trying to find my life and hope in anything other than You. Open my eyes to Your goodness and love manifesting in my life today. Amen.

The Rewrite: Ourselves

RECOMMENDED BIBLE READING:
Galatians 5:13-26

Today we are going to examine the language we use with ourselves. Because God is a reconciling God, He is always working to bring wholeness and integration in our lives— from the inside out. Jesus said, "Out of the abundance of the heart the mouth speaks" (Matthew 12:34, ESV). How we speak to ourselves in our heart will have a direct impact in how we perceive the external world.

Here are three translations of Galatians 5:22-23. Notice the words given for what we should expect the Holy Spirit to produce in our lives:

New Living Translation

The Holy Spirit produces this kind of fruit in our lives: love, joy, peace, patience, kindness, goodness, faithfulness, gentleness, and self-control.

The Message

What happens when we live God's way? He brings gifts into our lives, much the same way that fruit appears in an orchard—things like affection for others, exuberance about life, serenity. We develop a willingness to stick with things, a sense of compassion in the heart, and a conviction that a basic holiness permeates things and people. We find ourselves involved in loyal commitments, not needing to force our way in life, able to marshal and direct our energies wisely.

Amplified Bible

The fruit of the Spirit [the result of His presence within us] is love [unselfish concern for others], joy, [inner] peace, patience [not the ability to wait, but how we act while waiting], kindness, goodness, faithfulness, gentleness, self-control.

1. List the fruit of the Spirit below:

   -                           •
   -                           •
   -                           •
   -                           •
   -

2. Does the voice you use *with yourself* manifest the fruit of the Spirit? Is your inner voice loving, joyful, peaceful,

kind? Is your inner voice patient with you, good to you, faithful to you, gentle in tone and words?

3. If the answer is no, why not? What do you fear would happen if you treated yourself with the same kindness that God treats you with?

Most of us hold tightly to our inner critic because we are fearful that without it, we will off-ramp into laziness and pride. But we aren't replacing our inner critic with a spoiled, self-centered child. We are replacing our inner dialogue with the voice of our heavenly Father.

Psychologist Ethan Kross led an experiment on how people can influence their inner voices. He found one simple shift—referring to themselves in third person—led people to be kinder to themselves.[12] To close your reflection today, take the following promises of God and insert your name to make them personal.

See what great love the Father has lavished on
_____, that _____ is called a child of
God!

The Lord takes delight in _____; he crowns [her/
him] with victory.

The Lord set his affection on _____ and loved
[her/him].

If your response to these promises is skepticism or flat-out denial, you'll need to put some work in to believe them. Consider writing these out, or posting them on your bathroom mirror or as your wallpaper on your phone. Keep repeating the truth until you believe it!

The Rewrite: Others

RECOMMENDED BIBLE READING:
Ephesians 4:1-16

Today we look at the work of rewriting our relationship with others. To grow in the way we love others in our new story, let's focus on our understanding of humility, sincerity, and grace.

Humility
Romans 12:3

By the grace given me I say to every one of you:
Do not think of yourself more highly than you ought,
but rather think of yourself with sober judgment, in
accordance with the faith God has distributed to each
of you.

The definition of humility, in its simplest form, is the accurate assessment of ourselves. The expression of the gospel in our lives is *honesty with self, boldness with Christ.* To practice humility is to use your own power and position for the good of others, not for your own gain. How might you practice humility today?

Sincerity

1 Peter 1:22

Now that you have purified yourselves by obeying the truth so that you have sincere love for each other, love one another deeply, from the heart.

In Scripture, the Greek word used for *sincere* means "inexperienced in the art of acting."[13] To be sincere is to speak honestly, vulnerably, and directly with others. It means exhibiting self-control—sticking with what you've said, apologizing when needed, and yielding to others, seeking first to understand. Who can you choose to practice sincerity with this week?

Grace

To be a person of grace has both a proactive and reactive side. On the proactive side, people of grace see words as powerful tools of encouragement, healing, and love.

What is the result of grace in the following verse?

Acts 20:32

Now I commit you to God and to the word of his grace, which can build you up and give you an inheritance among all those who are sanctified.

On the reactive side, people of grace actively ask for forgiveness and seek reconciliation on a daily basis. Challenge yourself today to actively seek forgiveness when needed.

Make your apology humble and sincere, applying what you've learned above. Do not defend your actions or debase yourself. Simply admit your wrong sincerely and ask for forgiveness (as opposed to using false apologies such as "you'll have to forgive me" or "I'm sorry you felt that way").

If you haven't flexed your apology muscle, this will feel difficult and awkward at first. Yet grace is the primary fruit of our rewritten relationship with God, so it's worth the work. *Practice this discipline!*

Day 5
The Rewrite: The World

RECOMMENDED BIBLE READING:
John 3:16-21

On days 1 through 4 we looked at how being transformed by God requires giving ourselves to God and actively renewing our minds. This transformation is reflected in our new stories. Today we will look at how the fruit of our transformed stories will manifest in a rewritten relationship with the world. Theologian Karl Barth said, "Take your Bible and take your newspaper, and read both. But interpret newspapers from your Bible."[14]

1. When you see tragic or dark news in the media, what's your response?

Most of us have compassion fatigue when we engage deeply with the world. We are overwhelmed by so much information, so much detail, and the graphic and violent images that fill our screen. It will be a great challenge to your faith to follow Barth's admonition to "interpret newspapers from your Bible."

2. Today, I encourage you to be a theologian—to seek a way forward in the darkness of the news in light of the gospel. Look up the following verses and record words that will help you find encouragement and hope in the midst of hardship:

Isaiah 25:8

Micah 6:8

Philippians 3:17-20

Revelation 21:3-4

3. What do these passages teach you about how to live in this world?

As we close this week, take heart in the following truth: God is actively and intentionally seeking to restore and redeem your story. As you begin to live into that truth, your language changes. What was a language of pride, condemnation, and fear becomes a language of love—toward God, toward yourself, toward others, and toward the world.

This love is not a greeting-card kind of love. It's fierce, demanding, passionate, and relentless. It requires sacrifice and energy and strength. It will demand more of you than you can give—and that is the point where you will discover the strength of Christ. Your life will become a passionate love story of God working in you and through you to make you the salt of the earth and light of the world. Let it be so! Amen!

Father, Your Word tells me that You are seeking those who would worship You in spirit and truth (John 4:24). You say that You are constantly looking for those who are devoted to You (2 Chronicles 16:9). Father, help me to believe that You are seeking me even as I am seeking You. Amen.

Session Six

Transitions

In every moment, between every line,

may your new story point to Jesus, who holds

every hardship and orchestrates every joy.

The Struggle Is Real, conclusion, page 250

There's a little piece of us that wants to believe that when we choose to live for Christ, we will be rewarded with an all-joy, no-pain life. But the reality of this world is that we will all face times of confusion, pain, and loss.

Our faith is tested most deeply in times that feel the most dark. How do we continue to live in freedom when life isn't going the way we planned? In order to hold on to the new story, we have to deal with the chapters we wish weren't written. Let's turn our hearts together to finding the joy of Christ even in our darkest days.

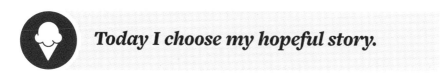 ***Today I choose my hopeful story.***

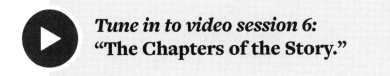

Tune in to video session 6:
"The Chapters of the Story."

Video Notes

Transitions test our character.

There's a difference between grief and guilt.

Out of the deep shadow of grief, something new can grow.

We experience our days in *chronos*, but our story is written in *kairos* moments.

Casey and Ashley's Story

"What I have to do is wake up, get out of bed every morning, and make the decision to trust the Lord in this. I can't control what happens to my body, but I can always control what happens in me . . . and in me, I choose to trust the Lord." —Casey

 **Reflection**

1. What resonates with you from Nicole's teaching or Casey and Ashley's story?

2. Have you experienced difficult waiting? What did you learn during that time?

3. How have you handled transitions? Have you experienced the confusion of grief and guilt?

4. Describe a recent *kairos* moment you've experienced.

📖 In the Word

Transitions test our faith. In seasons of uncertainty, we have to dig deep into our stories to hold tightly to the truth. In our humanity, we falter, but God is steady and faithful. Let's look at some examples from Scripture.

1. Turn to Matthew 11:1-3. What question does John the Baptist ask of Jesus?

2. Turn to John 6:60-70 and read it closely. What three questions does Jesus ask His disciples in this passage?

   •

   •

   •

In both of these passages, we see men of great faith—the men closest to Jesus—experiencing doubt.

3. Turn to John 1:22-34. How would you describe John the Baptist's faith?

4. This does not sound like the same man who, from prison, asks Jesus the question from Matthew 11! Based on these passages, what happens to John in his uncertainty?

5. In John 6:67, Jesus asks his closest friends a tender and vulnerable question: "You do not want to leave too, do you?" What is Peter's response?

 Application

1. Remember session 2, where we talked about the enemy's strategy to call into doubt the intentions of God? Do you tend to doubt God's intentions in difficult seasons? Why?

2. Hebrews 3:12-14 gives us strategies for weathering storms of doubt. If you were counseling a friend in a difficult season, what words of truth would you share? Write one or two sentences of truth for difficult seasons:

The joy of this exercise is that the words we would use for others can become instructive for our own soul. Consider writing the encouragement from Hebrews 3:12-14 on a 3 x 5 card and posting it on your mirror or dashboard where you'll see it often.

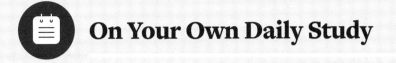 # On Your Own Daily Study

THIS WEEK'S RECOMMENDED READING:
***Chapter 10 and the conclusion in* The Struggle
Is Real**

For our final week of this series, we turn our attention to integrating all we've learned into our new story. Let's review what we've learned each week:

> Life is a choice—choose wisely!
> The struggle starts the story.
> At just the right time—Jesus.
> The past impacts but does not define my future.
> Wisdom takes work—and it's worth it.

We will also look at our story in relation to *kairos* time— moments of opportunity that matter to the deeper parts of our story. We seize those opportunities when we follow God as He invites us to experience His fullness every day, even in the most difficult seasons of life.

Day 1
The Choice

RECOMMENDED BIBLE READING:
Deuteronomy 30:11-20

Read the following verses to remind you of our first premise that *life is a choice*:

Deuteronomy 30:19-20

This day I call the heavens and the earth as witnesses against you that I have set before you life and death, blessings and curses. Now choose life, so that you and your children may live and that you may love the LORD your God, listen to his voice, and hold fast to him.

As you recall, these are Moses' words to the Israelites—his last exhortation to them as they were ready to cross into the Promised Land. Even though they were moving into what had been promised to them, they still had a choice to make. Choosing life meant loving and following God. Choosing death meant choosing anything other than God's way.

Fast-forward to the New Testament, and check out Jesus' words:

John 7:37-38

On the last and greatest day of the festival, Jesus stood and said in a loud voice, "Let anyone who is thirsty come to me and drink. Whoever believes in me, as Scripture has said, rivers of living water will flow from within them."

John 8:31-32

To the Jews who had believed him, Jesus said, "If you hold to my teaching, you are really my disciples. Then you will know the truth, and the truth will set you free."

1. In these passages, what is Jesus asking of people?

2. In session 1, you identified factors that sometimes prevent you from inviting God into your struggles. Have your interactions with God in the struggles changed? Why or why not?

3. What have you learned about "choosing life" with God daily?

Making the intentional, willful decision to "choose life" is something that we do every single day. To choose life is to choose God—to believe that He is highest, and He knows best.

Day 2
Good Desperation

RECOMMENDED BIBLE READING:
Mark 10:17-27

Today we focus on how *the struggle starts the story.*

1. Read Mark 10:17-22. As you read it, try imagining
    yourself in the story. First, read it from the vantage
    point of the man, then of Jesus, then of the crowd.
    What thoughts and feelings does engaging with this
    passage in this way bring up?

2. Read verse 26. What was the response of the disciples
    when they overheard Jesus' interchange with the man
    and His remarks to them after the man had gone away
    (see verses 23-25)?

Matthew 5 is a record of Jesus' Sermon on the Mount, which has been called the greatest sermon ever preached. In this message, Jesus explained much about the Kingdom of God.

Matthew 5:3-6, MSG

You're blessed when you're at the end of your rope. With less of you there is more of God and his rule.

You're blessed when you feel you've lost what is most dear to you. Only then can you be embraced by the One most dear to you.

You're blessed when you're content with just who you are—no more, no less. That's the moment you find yourselves proud owners of everything that can't be bought.

You're blessed when you've worked up a good appetite for God. He's food and drink in the best meal you'll ever eat.

3. How do the blessings detailed here relate to the story in Mark 10?

4. If the struggle is the story, how have you grown through the struggle (either past or present)? On a scale of 1 to 10, how likely are you to fully surrender a struggle to God, knowing that "with man this is impossible, but not with God; all things are possible with God" (Mark 10:27)?

The struggle brings us to good desperation—a reminder of our utter dependence on God to meet us in our need.

Day 3
At Just the Right Time

RECOMMENDED BIBLE READING:
Selected passages from Hebrews below

Today we remember that *at just the right time—Jesus.*

Jesus is the hero of our story. The good news of Jesus is not something we cash in for a one-way ticket to heaven, but it is an ever-present reality that continues to redeem, restore, and bring us deep joy each day. But here's the thing—in the midst of the countless streams of information we are bombarded with, we can easily become confused about who we are and what Christ has really done for us. Let's review these truths together.

We are going to use the book of Hebrews as our backdrop for strengthening our belief that Jesus is the supreme, final, and complete answer for our Struggle and our salvation. Friends, you will never waste time in God's Word, and you will always be strengthened by the truth of salvation.

1. Read Hebrews 1:1-3. What is the job of the Son? Where is He now?

2. Read Hebrews 2:3-4. Who announced salvation? How was it testified to?

3. Read Hebrews 2:14-15. What did Jesus' death accomplish?

4. Read Hebrews 4:9-10. What do the people of God experience?

5. Read Hebrews 9:14-15. What did the blood of Christ accomplish?

6. Read Hebrews 9:28. What will happen when Christ returns?

7. Read Hebrews 12:1-3. What should we do in light of this good news?

Praise be to Jesus, the author of each of our stories. Romans 5:6 says, "At just the right time, when we were still powerless, Christ died for the ungodly." At just the right time, Jesus entered your story. At just the right time, His sacrifice means your salvation. At just the right time, His life becomes your life. Our only possible response to this news is worship! Amen!

The New Family

RECOMMENDED BIBLE READING:
Galatians 6:1-10 .

Today we remember that *the past impacts but does not define our future.*

1. When you think back to your reflections from session 4, what did you learn about yourself that still sticks with you most?

One of the incredible promises for all of us to discover is that in Christ we've been given a new family. Consider these two surprising passages from Luke:

Luke 8:19-21

Jesus' mother and brothers came to see him, but they were not able to get near him because of the crowd. Someone told him, "Your mother and brothers are standing outside, wanting to see you." He replied, "My mother and brothers are those who hear God's word and put it into practice."

Luke 9:61-62

Another said, "I will follow you, Lord; but first let me go back and say goodbye to my family." Jesus replied, "No one who puts a hand to the plow and looks back is fit for service in the kingdom of God."

2. Now we know that Jesus is perfect and without sin, so His response here is not disrespectful or disobedient. But what He is emphasizing is our priority. In these passages, what is *more* important than family?

Now read the following passages:

John 1:11-13

He came to that which was his own, but his own did not receive him. Yet to all who did receive him, to those who believed in his name, he gave the right to become children of God—children born not of natural descent, nor of human decision or a husband's will, but born of God.

Hebrews 2:11

Both the one who makes people holy and those who are made holy are of the same family. So Jesus is not ashamed to call them brothers and sisters.

3. What is the result of our life in Christ?

Praise God, who gives us a new family when we receive Jesus. Our earthly family remains important, but they no longer define our future. That is now secure in Christ, and we join the invisible church around the world—brothers and sisters who call Jesus their Savior and who have been given the right to become children of God.

Day 5
Growing through Transition

RECOMMENDED BIBLE READING:
1 Peter 1

Our last focus point is *wisdom takes work—and it's worth it.*

1. Last week, we looked at new language for our new story—rewriting our relationship with God, with ourselves, with others, and with the world. In which of those relationships do you feel strong? Where do you need the most growth?

One of the most challenging times to live into our new story is in transitions. We are going to look at three passages in Scripture that give a framework for navigating seasons of change.

Psalm 90:12

Teach us to number our days aright, that we may gain a heart of wisdom.

2. What would it look like for you to number your days correctly, with an accurate sense of the brevity of life? What would you do more of? Less of?

Now read the following passages from 1 Peter and James. Underline the purpose of trials:

1 Peter 1:6-9

In all this you greatly rejoice, though now for a little while you may have had to suffer grief in all kinds of trials. These have come so that the proven genuineness of your faith—of greater worth than gold, which perishes even though refined by fire—may result in praise, glory and honor when Jesus Christ is revealed. Though you have not seen him, you love him; and even though you do not see him now, you believe in him and are filled with an inexpressible and glorious joy, for you are receiving the end result of your faith, the salvation of your souls.

James 1:2-4

Consider it pure joy, my brothers and sisters, whenever you face trials of many kinds, because you know that the testing of your faith produces perseverance. Let perseverance finish its work so that you may be mature and complete, not lacking anything.

3. In both passages, trials and joy are linked to one another. Why do you think they go together?

4. As we close our time together, here is one last question—the most important one of the entire series. We all know that the struggle is real. My relentless prayer and deep hope for you now is that you also know why the struggle matters. In light of all you've experienced during this study, what *kairos* moments from your story do you cling to? In other words, what have you learned is important about your life?

The Hopeful Story Prayer

Gracious Father, just today:
Give me the courage to face reality.
Give me the grace to receive Your love in my
*   failings and Your affection in my weaknesses.*
Give me the strength to choose life—the way
*   You've made it.*

Jesus Christ,
I accept You as the Giver of Life.
I receive You as the Author of my soul.
And I choose You as my Lord.

Holy Spirit,
dwell in me, speak to me, walk with me,
that I may grow in wisdom, live in hope, and
*   rejoice in freedom today.*
AMEN!

Concluding Thoughts

We created this video series to reflect one day—one day of choices, one day of relationships, one day of struggle and joy. One day when the sun comes up, when we are free to make the choice to "choose life," to live into our new story in our thoughts, words, and actions. We live one day at a time, chronologically. We are bound by hours, days, calendars. We are subject to the forces of aging and gravity. Indeed, "outwardly we are wasting away," as the apostle Paul states so bluntly in 2 Corinthians 4:16.

But because of *kairos* moments—those opportune moments when we sense God is near and when we recognize that we are not just physical beings on a calendar but spiritual beings in eternity—we also live into the promise that continues in verse 16 above: "Though outwardly we are wasting away, inwardly we are being renewed day by day." Yes, on God's time line, your body may be getting older, but your spirit can be getting younger—full of vitality and strength, renewed in wonder, in joy, and in salvation.

What an incredible story God invites us to experience in our lives. When we are in Christ, the struggle is still real, but the war is won. Our enemy is defeated, and we no longer have to experience separation from God. What a wonder. What a joy. What a life.

If you've experienced the good news of Jesus for the first time through this study, we want to know! Nicole would love to send you a resource to help you take the next steps in your relationship with Christ. E-mail info@takeheartministry.com to share your story.

A Guide for Leaders

As the leader of a group, you are taking on a great work. You are now fulfilling the call to ministry that Jesus gives to every one of His followers. Jesus told us to be His witnesses to the work He's done in our lives, and to do that all the way to the ends of the earth! Your "end of the earth" might look like inviting your neighbors over for dessert—and that is awesome. God's plan A for reaching people with His message of love and life is *us*. You and me. *Us*—in the midst of all of our screwups, sin, fear, and limits, God delights in using us to share His good news. If you feel unworthy, unprepared, or just plain scared to lead a group, that's a great place to be. Second Corinthians 12:9 says, "My grace is sufficient for you, for my power is made perfect in weakness." His grace is sufficient, and He will provide what you need! Lift your weaknesses to Him and lift up your head. Now send out those invites—you are officially in ministry.

This guide will help you with the resources you need to launch and lead your group. You'll find answers to the questions leaders often ask below, followed by leaders' notes for each session.

Who should be in my group?

There is no perfect formula for a group. Any context that draws people together can be the basis for forming one. For you, this might look like an existing Bible study or Sunday school class. My hope is that it might look like a group of friends you usually work out with, a gathering of coworkers, or the moms from your child's soccer team. If some activity or group of people draws you together, you already have something in common.

The Struggle Is Real is written for anyone who wants a deeper understanding about how life works and what it means to be a wholehearted, wise person. Some questions may invite participants to be vulnerable about their struggles, but we've structured each session to give you multiple entry points—and sharing is always optional. So everyone's welcome—and hopefully there's a little bit of something for everyone in the study!

What do we need to get started?

Everyone in the group needs a copy of this participant's guide and a Bible for group time. We also recommend that members pick up a copy of *The Struggle Is Real* book, but it is not required for the study.

How long will each group session take?

The study is structured so that each session can be completed in ninety minutes. You may take longer if needed, but I've found that most people's attention begins to wane at this point. If you have less time, you can edit the questions and choose to move more of the group work to personal study time. Here is the suggested format:

10 minutes: Welcome and Connection Question
10 minutes: Observations from Daily Study*
20 minutes: Video Time
10 minutes: Reflection
20 minutes: In the Word
15 minutes: Application
5 minutes: Prayer

Do we need the book The Struggle Is Real?

The Struggle Is Real has three components: the book, the participant's guide, and the video experience. Consider the book like a personal conversation in which I draw stories from my own life and the lives of many others who have come into wholehearted living with Christ. In this guide, we take those truths and make them personal and interactive by opening the Bible together and walking through these life-changing principles. In the video, I've selected a few stories to tell— from personal friends of mine who've experienced what it

---

*In the notes for session 1, more time is given for the Welcome and Connection Question to allow group members adequate time to get to know one another. Because it will be your first meeting, no time is needed to discuss the Daily Study questions from the previous week.

means to walk in God's freedom. I also teach straight from the Bible in order to help you understand scriptural principles and discuss them with your friends.

You can use these resources in any order: You may read the book first and then reinforce your learning with the study, you can read the book as a companion to the study (I recommend which chapters to read during each session), or you can do the study on its own. It is best, however, to use this participant's guide *with* the video, as those two work together.

I don't know how to be a leader. Help!

If you are new to facilitating a group, rest assured that you are not alone. Everyone is intimidated when they first start leading a group. It can feel presumptuous to pretend that you are the spiritually mature one who is ready to "lead" your peers in Bible study! But have no fear—that's not the spirit of this study. To be a leader in *The Struggle Is Real* is to admit that you are a chief struggler—not someone who has arrived!

A great group leader doesn't need to have all the answers (in fact, that usually makes a person *not* a great leader). A great group leader does two things. One, the leader makes the group *safe*. *Safe* means the leader starts and ends on time, keeps the group on track with questions, and gently redirects if one group member is trying to give advice or "fix" someone else. Second, the leader makes the group *honest*. *Honest* means the leader is willing to be vulnerable when responding to the questions, creates space for people to share fully and openly, and encourages each member of the group to grow.

A group that has both safety and honesty is a setting where powerful development can happen.

Here are some other helpful hints as you lead your group:

- This study works equally well in a ministry setting, such as a larger group situated around tables, or in a home or small group setting.

- As the leader, you set the tone for the depth and authenticity of your group. Your job is not to have all the answers, but to be open so that people can come with questions and vulnerability and feel heard and understood. You do that by sharing from your own life and by giving others the space to share.

- You also set the tone through your own preparation. By previewing the video and working through the questions in the guide in advance, you'll have a better sense of what questions to focus on and how the group is likely to go each time you meet. Your preparation also tells your group that you value their time and expect this experience to be important and meaningful. Be sure to preview the leader guide for each week before the group meets, in case you need extra materials or preparation. The tone of the leader determines the tone of the group.

- Communication as a leader is key. Make sure you connect with your group between sessions via e-mail, text, etc., to clarify what the group should do to prepare for the next meeting and to remind them when and where you'll be meeting.

- Your group will most likely not have time to respond to every question during your time together—and that's okay! The questions fit into three categories: connecting with one another, knowing the Word, and applying the Word to life. Depending on the experiences of the people in the group, some of those categories may be more conducive to discussion than others. Try to hit at least one of the questions from each section every time you meet, but focus on what's best for the group.

- If you want more help in becoming a great group leader, check out the leader resources at nicoleunice. com/leaders.

My prayer is that you experience surprising refreshment in the Lord as you serve so that you can refresh others. I pray that God will bless you with wisdom and compassion for the people in the group—and perhaps in new ways for yourself. And "I pray that you, being rooted and established in love, may have power, together with all the Lord's holy people, to grasp how wide and long and high and deep is the love of Christ" (Ephesians 3:17-18). Amen!

Session 1

The following guidelines are meant to help you manage your time and get the most out of your group. Remember, these instructions are intended to give you confidence as you get to know your group members and respond to what works best for them. It's said that 90 percent of leadership is just showing up, so show up for your group—be fully present, be fully yourself, and pray that God will use your faithfulness to bring Him glory. It's a prayer He loves to answer.

Session 1 Goal

To establish the rhythm of your group, create a comfortable environment and make initial connections with one another.

Welcome (10 minutes)

Make sure everyone knows one another's names. Go over the basics: stage of life, workplace, what drew the person to the group. Don't forget to share what prompted you to start or lead the group! (Note: For session 1 only, I suggest planning for a slightly extended welcome time to allow for group introductions. In the guidelines for sessions 2 through 6, the Welcome and Connection Question are combined.)

Connection Question (10 minutes)

Even if your group members already know each other well, connection time is a chance to find out something new, to hear something different, and to allow space for old friends to surprise one another with new details! If your group members don't know one another well or at all, this time is *crucial* because it gives everyone a chance to be themselves without the intimidation of jumping right into a conversation about spiritual things. I'll always provide direction, but feel free to make this time your own.

> *Much of our time together will involve looking back at our lives in order to look forward to our future. To start, choose one year of elementary school to describe to the group. Where did you live? What did you love? Who were you around? Describe a favorite toy, outfit, sport, or hobby.*

Video Time (20 minutes)
Tune in to session 1. Make sure everyone knows they can take notes in their guide as they listen.

Reflection (10 minutes)
Consult session 1 in your guide for questions that follow the video content. You may not be able to answer every one in the time you have, so pick one or two to focus on and then return to this section if you have extra time.

In the Word (20 minutes)
This time is designed to help everyone get comfortable exploring the Bible together. It can be helpful to have an extra Bible handy so you can pass it around and read aloud.

Application (15 minutes)
This is the takeaway—where it gets real. If you run out of time, feel free to share your own answer to the Application question as a way to set the tone of honesty for the group.

Prayer (5 minutes)

In the first session, it's best for you to close in prayer. As you get to know your group, you can move to sharing prayer requests and then praying together. Be mindful of those in your group who are exploring faith or are new to faith. Avoid "Christianese"—the tendency for Christians to use terms that those new to the faith don't understand. Pray sincerely and simply, and you'll help others learn to approach God in the same way.

Don't forget to close your time by covering the basics—when and where you'll meet next, an encouragement to complete the homework, and a reminder to bring a Bible next time. You may wish to get everyone's contact information and follow up with a simple individual text in the next couple of days. ("Hey, Terry! So glad you joined us for our first group. I really enjoyed what you shared about your third grade teacher. Looking forward to seeing you next time!")

Simple communication and follow-up helps each person in your group feel known and cared for, which goes a *long* way!

Session 2

Session 2 Goal

To go one level deeper in connection, to become comfortable discussing biblical truths, to share honestly from the homework.

Welcome and Connection Question (10 minutes)

Here's a possible question to get your group started:

What do you collect? Some of us collect physical items or memorabilia. Others collect memories, achievements, or relationships. Share a story about something you've collected over the years and what it means to you.

Observations from Session 1 Daily Study

(10 minutes)

As a way to grow together and stay accountable, open your session with feedback from the week's homework. It can be helpful to give some clear prompts:

Let's take a couple of minutes to look back over our notes from last week. Underline any reflection that stuck out for you that you can share.

This creates an easy way for people to participate without feeling lost in the homework, not sure where to start. This also allows those who could not complete the homework to draw on the previous video session if they prefer.

Video Time (20 minutes)

Tune in to session 2. Make sure everyone knows they can take notes in their guide as they listen.

Reflection (10 minutes)

Consult session 2 in your guide for questions that follow the video content (page 25). You may not be able to answer every one in the time you have, so pick one or two to focus on and then return to this section if you have extra time. Make sure to allow time for each person to fill out the inventory located here.

In the Word (20 minutes)

The content should be easy to follow and not take too long to complete—but dealing with the truth of sin and our role in it can be a difficult conversation! Remember, as the leader it's not your job to have all the answers. Talking deeply about brokenness can lead to people sharing honestly about their frustration or confusion with God. It's okay simply to allow thoughts to be shared without trying to defend God or answer for Him.

Be sure to redirect the conversation if anyone in the group tries to hit someone with well-meaning but unhelpful advice or begins asking detailed questions in an attempt to "fix" anyone's problems. When that happens, consider saying something like, "Suzy, it sounds like you might have some great things to share. I'm sure if Greg hasn't tried that, he could follow up with you after group time if he would like. I would love to make sure we get to hear from everyone, so let's get back to the questions."

Application (15 minutes)

This is the takeaway—where it gets real. This week's application encourages a response to the teaching on sin and brokenness. Depending on the comfort level of your group, you may need to help people open up. One idea is to refer back to Erin's story from the video and talk about the things we've believed about ourselves that are lies.

Prayer (5 minutes)

If your group is ready for it, this is a great time to pray for one another. You can do this by inviting your group to pair up and share one request that the other person can pray about in the upcoming week. If the group is uncomfortable with that, you could also pick one person to open in prayer and then you could close your prayer time.

It's always helpful to encourage your group to do the homework and remind them of the time and place you'll meet for session 3.

Session 3

Session 3 Goal

To connect the character of God and the work of Jesus to our own understanding of freedom. To explore together what "freedom" looks like in our daily lives.

Welcome and Connection Question (10 minutes)

Here's a possible question to get your group started:

> *Describe where and when you feel free (of obligations, concerns, duties, etc.). What's different about you when you experience freedom? What keeps you from experiencing that more frequently?*

Observations from Session 2 Daily Study

(10 minutes)

As a way to grow together and stay accountable, open your session with feedback from the week's homework. Your group should be more comfortable now sharing freely.

> *Looking back on your reflections from last week, what's something new you've discovered about yourself?*

> *Do you have any follow-up comments or questions from our homework last week?*

Video Time (20 minutes)

Tune in to session 3. This week is heavier on the "teaching" section, so feel free to rewind or watch the freedom cycle section again.

Reflection (10 minutes)

Consult session 3 in your guide for questions that follow the video content. You may not be able to answer every one in the time you have, so pick one or two to focus on and then return to this section if you have extra time.

In the Word (20 minutes)

Today we look at a story that may be familiar to some—but ask God to spark your imagination to see it afresh!

Application (15 minutes)

Depending on your group's vulnerability, you might want to ask if anyone can share about a memory or moment when they have felt condemned (by themselves or others). If the group isn't ready for that, you might pass out a 3 x 5 card to each member in the group. Then ask them to write down a struggle, fold it, and then exchange cards in the group. Once each person has another's card, have them tear up the card without reading what's written on it. Then have that person tell the other, "Neither do I condemn you." Talk about the experience together. What did it feel like when the other person held your "sin" in their hands? What did it feel like when it was ripped up?

Prayer (5 minutes)

You may ask the group if they have any Scriptures or ways to pray that help them when they are feeling stuck in anything *but* freedom. If you want the group to grow in prayer together, you could start prayer by having the group turn to a psalm and then asking each person to read one verse out loud, after which you pray in closing. That helps "break the ice" in prayer.

It's always helpful to encourage your group to make time to do the upcoming homework. This week we make the crossover from looking back at our story to looking ahead—and we get really practical about how we live our freedom story!

 # Session 4

Session 4 Goal

This week, we focus on exploring our family foundations. For some, this will be a familiar exercise—for others, it can be emotional and difficult. I encourage you, as the leader of your group, to pray for each person by name this week. Ask God to give you discernment and wisdom to create an environment of vulnerability and grace.

Welcome and Connection Question (10 minutes)

Here are two questions you can use to get your group started:

What's something from your growing-up family that you want to take into your future? What's something that you want to leave behind?

Looking back on your study of God's character last week, what's something you've discovered about Him?

Observations from Session 3 Daily Study

(10 minutes)

Look back on your reflections from last week and briefly discuss the story themes you uncovered.

What freedom derailers have you noticed yourself falling into this week? How do you get yourself back on the freedom cycle?

Video Time (20 minutes)

Tune in to session 4.

Reflection (10 minutes)

Consult session 4 in your guide for questions that follow the video content. You may not be able to answer every one in the time you have, so pick one or two to focus on and then return to this section if you have extra time. Make sure to allow time for each person to fill out the inventory located here.

In the Word (20 minutes)

Today we look at how we can expect to hear from God. Share together about your experiences of hearing (or not hearing!) God's voice. How can we discern God's voice among the many voices we hear in our hearts and minds?

Application (15 minutes)

The idea of hearing from God can feel as if it's reserved for the superspiritual or mystics among us. But Scripture makes clear that God speaks—drawing us into worship, into truth, and into the good works "which God prepared in advance for us to do" (Ephesians 2:10). He speaks to us through His creation, through other believers, and through His Word. Close your time together by spending a few minutes in silence, asking for God's leading and bringing each person in the group before God. Jot down any specific encouragement for others in the group that comes to mind. Then share that as you close your time.

Prayer (5 minutes)

A closing prayer:

God of mercy, heal our broken places, rewrite our difficult memories, and give us the courage and strength to be resurrected in all ways by Your grace. Amen.

As we move toward our final weeks, encourage your group to continue the habit of working through their daily homework. Remind them to keep an open and attentive mind to the way God is showing up in their past and reshaping their present.

Session 5

Session 5 Goal

This week, we uncover the words of our inner world—and the work it takes to rewrite our story. It might be fun this week to play a game of Charades or Heads Up! (available as a free or very low cost app for your smartphone) as a way to start your time—something that makes your group think about how they do (or don't) use words to get their meaning across.

Welcome and Connection Question (10 minutes)

Here's a possible question to get your group started:

> *As a kid, did you have any irrational fears? Where did those fears come from? How did you grow out of them?*

Observations from Session 4 Daily Study (10 minutes)

Look back on your reflections from day 4 ("The Power of Self-Examination") last week. What's something you learned about yourself?

Video Time (20 minutes)

Tune in to session 5.

Reflection (10 minutes)

Consult session 5 in your guide for questions that follow the video content. You may not be able to answer every one in the time you have, so pick one or two to focus on and then return to this section if you have extra time.

In the Word (20 minutes)

Today we talk about the way we rewrite our relationship with ourselves, with others, and with the world. One of the hardest relationship realities is the delicate balance between grace and truth. When do we speak up, and when do we hold our tongue? As your group is comfortable, one or more might want to share about a situation they are trying to work through in this "rewrite" category. Encourage your group to listen and ask questions, but try to steer away from advice giving and solutions. You may find this to be a great exercise in healthy listening for the whole group!

Application (15 minutes)

As your group members consider where their faith foundations may need to be strengthened, this may be a good time to challenge one another to make a commitment this week to a change of mind, such as

- listening for their inner critic and replacing criticism with love,
- choosing a Scripture to memorize and repeat when feeling anxious, or
- listening for a voice of gossip, judgment, or complaint and choosing to stop exercising that voice for a week.

Prayer (5 minutes)

A prayer to close your time:

God of strength, we cannot rewrite these well-worn scripts in our own strength. Holy Spirit, give us the power and ability to choose the truth. Would You help us to believe and live out of the knowledge of Your love for us? Then help us to impact those around us with that same love. Amen.

Session 6

Session 6 Goal

We have one more important aspect of the new story to discover: holding on to our new story when we face transitions. Transitions come in the inevitable changes of season as well as in the unexpected, the difficult, and even the tragic circumstances that may come our way.

Welcome and Connection Question (10 minutes)

Here's a possible question to get your group started:

> *Describe one year of your life that was particularly meaningful. What aspects contributed to that experience?*

Observations from Session 5 Daily Study

(10 minutes)

You may open the conversation regarding the past week with the question from day 3's homework: "Does the voice you use *with yourself* manifest the fruit of the Holy Spirit?" Talk together about why (if it's true for your group) we tend to be harsher with ourselves than we are with others.

Video Time (20 minutes)

Tune in to session 6.

Reflection (10 minutes)

Consult session 6 in your guide for questions that follow the video content. You may not be able to answer every one in the time you have, so pick one or two to focus on and then return to this section if you have extra time.

In the Word (20 minutes)

As you work through the Bible study content, discuss how you handle seasons of doubt—both your own and those of other people. Why does doubt make us uncomfortable? What would it look like to embrace seasons of difficulty— either your own or a loved one's?

Application (15 minutes)

We've covered a lot of ground in our last sessions. What has been the most meaningful for where you are in your story?

Close your time by giving one another the specific gift of encouragement. Hand each person in the group a note card or a piece of paper, and have them write their name at the top. Then have participants pass their papers to their right. Once they've taken a sheet from the person sitting next to them, they should add a verse, sentence, or specific word of encouragement about how they've seen the named person grow in the past six weeks. Keep passing the papers until each person has had a chance to add something to each card. At the end, everyone will have a page of encouragement to remind them of the growth they've experienced through this study.

Prayer (5 minutes)

Psalm 107:2 says, "Let the redeemed of the LORD tell their story." Close your time together by offering a prayer for courage and confidence for each group member to live (and tell!) their redeemed stories.

Notes

1. Sally Clarkson, *Own Your Life* (Carol Stream, IL: Tyndale House, 2014), 163.
2. Thomas Watson, *The Doctrine of Repentance* (1668).
3. *Oxford Dictionary Online*, s.v. "cherish," https://en.oxforddictionaries.com /definition/cherish.
4. Brennan Manning, *Ruthless Trust: The Ragamuffin's Path to God* (New York: HarperCollins, 2010, reprint edition), 73.
5. *Merriam-Webster's Collegiate Dictionary*, 11th ed., s.v. "redeem" (bold added for emphasis).
6. Dallas Willard, *Hearing God: Developing a Conversational Relationship with God* (Downers Grove, IL: IVP, 2012), 42, italics in the original.
7. *Strong's Concordance*, s.v. "holos," http://biblehub.com/greek/3650.htm.
8. David G. Benner, *The Gift of Being Yourself: The Sacred Call to Self-Discovery* (Downers Grove, IL: IVP, 2015), 17.
9. *The Later Lectures of Ralph Waldo Emerson: 1843–1871*, ed. Ronald A. Bosco and Joel Myerson, vol. 2, *1855–1871* (Athens, GA: University of Georgia Press, 2010), 363.
10. Charles Haddon Spurgeon, "On Laying Foundations," sermon presented at Metropolitan Tabernacle, Newington, England, January 21, 1883, http:// www.spurgeongems.org/vols28-30/chs1702.pdf.
11. Caroline Leaf, *Switch On Your Brain: The Key to Peak Happiness, Thinking, and Health* (Grand Rapids: Baker, 2013), https://www.goodreads.com /work/quotes/26928437-switch-on-your-brain-the-key-to-peak-happiness -thinking-and-health.
12. Laura Starecheski, "Why Saying Is Believing—The Science of Self-Talk," *NPR*, October 7, 2014, http://www.npr.org/sections/health-shots/2014 /10/07/353292408/why-saying-is-believing-the-science-of-self-talk.
13. *Hebrew-Greek Key Word Study Bible*, NIV edition, s.v. "anypokritos."
14. "Barth in Retirement," *Time* magazine, May 31, 1963, http://content.time .com/time/subscriber/article/0,33009,896838,00.html.

About the Author

Nicole Unice is an author and Bible teacher who has a passion for bringing God's Word to life in a personal and relevant way. Her training as a counselor informs her work, as she emphasizes the importance of facing our own reality and embracing the transforming power of God's grace.

Invitations to speak have taken Nicole around the world, and her books come to life through her popular video curriculum series found on RightNow Media. Her heart belongs to Hope Church in Richmond, Virginia, where she serves as ministry director and leads Praxis, a full-time ministry residency program for young leaders.

Nicole holds degrees from the College of William and Mary and from Gordon-Conwell Theological Seminary. She loves creating space for spiritual growth in the everyday rhythms of life with three children, two pups, one husband, and a whole community of twentysomethings who regularly raid her fridge.

If life seems harder than it should,

get ready to find new strength and confidence! Join popular Bible teacher and counselor Nicole Unice to discover why the struggle is real . . . and what to do about it.

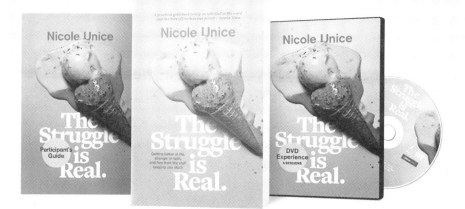

The Struggle Is Real Participant's Guide: This is a six-session workbook designed for use with *The Struggle Is Real DVD Experience*, based on the book by Nicole Unice. A great resource for church groups, Bible studies, and anyone who's ever felt life just shouldn't be this hard!

The Struggle Is Real: Nicole Unice provides practical tools to help you navigate daily ups and downs and offers ways to rewrite your struggle into a new, God-centered life story. Discover how to take the hard, hurtful, and confusing moments and turn them into opportunities to grow in wisdom, strength, and joy.

The Struggle Is Real DVD Experience: Designed for use with *The Struggle Is Real Participant's Guide*, this six-session DVD curriculum, based on Nicole Unice's book, teaches how to practice gratitude, make godly choices, and live each day with confidence and contentment. Also available through online streaming at www.rightnowmedia.org.

To learn more from Nicole and access additional resources, visit her online at www.nicoleunice.com.

THE EVERYDAY STUFF THAT DRIVES YOU CRAZY . . . IS ABOUT TO TRANSFORM YOUR LIFE.

Some days living up to the whole good-Christian thing seems impossible. You do the right things (well, most of the time), but you just don't feel changed by your faith. Deep down, you're still dealing with the everyday issues—control, insecurity, comparison, fear, and anger (along with its cousin, unforgiveness)—that hold you back from living free and loving well.

The good news? You don't have to "fix" yourself. You have access to the power of Christ. His power can transform your everyday weaknesses into your greatest strengths and gifts. In *She's Got Issues*, you'll join Christian counselor, ministry leader, and regular mom Nicole Unice on a new journey of learning to better understand yourself and others by exploring how these issues affect us . . . and why we don't have to settle for letting them win.

Bring *Brave Enough* to your
community, and start living

BOLD and FREE

Brave Enough

Find the courage to be who
you are . . . not who you wish
you were. Discover what it
means to live a brave-enough
life, fully alive and confident
in who God made you to be.

978-1-4964-0136-6

Brave Enough DVD Group Experience

Join Nicole on an eight-week
journey to being brave enough
right where you are.

978-1-4964-0138-0